Reclaiming Afrikan

QUEER PERSPECTIVES ON SEXUAL AND GENDER IDENTITIES

CURATED BY
ZETHU MATEBENI

This publication was made possible by Hivos
This Iranti-org project is funded by Arcus Foundation

First published by Modjaji Books Pty Ltd
PO Box 385, Athlone, 7760, South Africa
modjaji.books@gmail.com
www.modjajibooks.co.za
ISBN 978-1-920590-49-9

Language editor: Karen Jennings
Design and layout: Louise Topping

Front cover image by Jabu C. Pereira
Back cover image by Kelebogile Ntladi

CONTENTS

FOREWORD

I am honoured that the editors of this bold set of essays and images have asked me to write this foreword. *Reclaiming Afrikan* forcefully intervenes in several significant debates. First, it joins essential books, such as *African Sexualities* edited by Sylvia Tamale, *Queer African Reader* edited by Sokari Ekine and Hakima Abbas, and *Queer Africa* compiled and edited by Karen Martin and Makhosazana Xaba, in exposing the hideous myth that queer sex is anti-African. Like those books, *Reclaiming Afrikan* acts as a rallying cry against the rapidly-spreading, vicious homophobia marching across the African continent. More than ever, we need these kinds of organising tools that help us strike back at attempts to isolate queer, sexual and gender non-conforming Africans from each other and larger communities. This is a terrifying isolation that leads to living in deeply-buried closets, flight into exile and, even torture and death. This cutting-edge book offers language and historical examples that we all can use to counter this march of homophobia.

Reclaiming Afrikan also speaks to international debates about queer behaviours around the world. By selectively engaging western theorists, such as Judith Butler and Eve Kosofsky Sedgwick, and African scholars, such as Binyavanga Wainaina and Keguro Macharia, several articles help create dialogues that will enrich us all. This engagement also makes it clear that African homophobia isn't some uniquely African condition.

As a Black American, I am particularly appreciative of the ways *Reclaiming Afrikan* speaks to debates throughout the African diaspora. I'm not talking here about diaspora ties that go back to the slave trade and mysteriously bind us all together. Rather I am concerned about what we face together now: the present day racists, sexists and homophobes who have tried to stir up homophobia both in Africa and the Americas. It has been well-established that US right-wing Christian groups have helped mobilise politicians in countries such as Uganda and Nigeria to create legislation targeting sexual and non-gender conforming citizens. The coalitions between these conservative politicians and western-based Christian groups who come with money to distribute have helped divert attention from more critical issues like poverty, sexism, and corruption.

Right-wing Christian groups have used the same tactics among black Americans. For example, these groups have helped fund conservative black preachers such as anti-gay Rev. William Owens and his Coalition of African-American Pastors (Madhani, n.pag.). The Christian Right has had mixed success in Black communities largely because Black Americans can see through their homophobia to their deep-rooted racism. Owens, for example, has failed to emerge as a credible leader.

But the right-wingers continue to try. Even the infamous Scott Lively, who has exported homophobia around the world, most notoriously to Uganda, has recently moved to Springfield, Massachusetts. Never a man to shun the limelight, he is recruiting followers from the large Black and Latino communities with platforms designed "to restore respect for marriage and the natural family". His attack on Obama as a "radical homosexualist" reveals that he is working in the service of the right-wing anti-Obama forces (The Griot n.pag.).

Reclaiming Afrikan is an ingenious collection of art, activism, and scholarship. While there is much to worry about in facing increasingly vocal homophobia, this book by its very existence makes room for optimism. And its content will leave you able to imagine a world in which we no longer have to struggle to protect queer, sexual and gender non-conforming Afrika.

Professor E Frances White
Gallatin School of Individualized Study and
Department of Social and Cultural Analysis,
New York University

REFERENCES

Madhani, Aamer. "Black pastors group has deep conservative ties, records show". *USA Today*. 8 October 2012. Web. 10 April 2014.

theGriot.com 2 April 2014. Web. 10 April 2014.

Self Portraits: *Dragonfly City* ▲
Acrylic on Canvas, (150 x 100 cm) 2010
This is Dragonfly City in a country called
Androgynous. Some kind of freakish,
awesome, perilous state to be.

Milumbe Haimbe

▲ *Keep Your Kobo Kobo Series*

Tyna Adebowale

PREFACE

The last few years have been deeply challenging for sexual and gender non-conforming persons in Africa. Various laws, legislations, traditional and religious fundamentalism have been strengthened in order to police and regulate non-normative sexualities and gender identities. Colonial laws introduced penal codes, commonly known as sodomy laws that criminalised so-called "unnatural" sexual acts. We have seen how these laws continue to exist in postcolonial times – having been upheld and promoted most recently in the early 1990s by the Zimbabwean president's anti-homophobic outbreaks, trickling to neighbouring countries and to the Eastern and Western horns of the continent. In some countries (current examples include Uganda, Gambia and Nigeria), such legislation aims to do away with people deemed homosexual and transsexual – either through imprisonment, death penalties or harsh social conditions such as ostracism, rape or even murder.

At the forefront of such social exclusion and legal policing are ideas perpetuated by many African political, religious and traditional leaders who argue that the only way to exist in the continent and to be recognised is by being heterosexual. This is against the rich histories and existence of people with diverse sexual orientations and practices in Africa. For mainly socio-political reasons, such leaders have considered homosexuality in Africa as "unAfrican". The language of religion, culture and tradition is often used to speak against sexual and gender diversity in the continent. Within this problematic framework, Africans are and can only be reproductive heterosexuals.

We live in a rich, diverse and dynamic continent. There are more than fifty countries in Africa. Nigeria alone has a population of more than 160 million. There is a wide range of racial, ethnic, cultural and linguistic groups as well as an assortment of sexual experiences, expressions and identities in this continent. How certain groups of people, who apart from ideology share very little else in common, would believe that the only way to be in this diverse place is singular, suggests blinkered thinking. Many of us who are located in this place called Africa feel a strong connection with the fabric of this continent – its richness, dynamism and diversity. This is what we embody.

In putting together this volume, *Reclaiming Afrikan: queer perspectives on sexual and gender identities*, we sought voices from the continent that bring new ideas to our diverse ways of existing. Many of the people in this volume see themselves as queer – a category that we are yet to recognise fully and understand in this continent. We appropriate both Afrika and queer to affirm sexual and gender identities and positions that are ordinarily shamed and violated by prejudice and hatred. Afrika itself is always detached from a queer person.

We deliberately use "k" in Afrikan to emphasise the need to *reclaim* our existence and being in this continent. As sexual and gender non-conforming or queer persons, we have been alienated in Africa. We have been stripped of our belonging and our connectedness. For these reasons, we have created our own version of Afrika – a space that cuts across the rigid borders and boundaries that have for so many years made us feel disconnected and fractured.

Reclaiming Afrikan brings us back together as artists, activists, scholars and writers from the different parts of the world we live in. It opens up a conversation for us to rewrite the ways in which we exist as people who move around this continent and beyond. We break borders, and even beyond these borders – we share a sense of kinship – a belonging to a struggle for freedom and social justice. We are, in many ways, queer in the queer sense of the term.

"Queer" in this book is understood as an inquiry into the present, as a critical space that pushes the boundaries of what is embraced as normative. The queer artists and authors included in *Reclaiming Afrikan* occupy spaces that speak back to hegemony. For many, this position challenges various norms on gender, sexuality, existence and offers a subversive way of being. Stella Nyanzi makes this clear in her essay when she asks us to think about the ways in which queer can be queered. If we are to use this term and embrace it, what does it mean for many whose experiences are constantly challenging norms? Can we even challenge the norm of what we see as queer – as it exists in the continent?

While we use the term *queer*, we are conscious of its polemics. Zethu Matebeni cynically argues that in the South African case queer has become synonymous with another problematic term, LGBTI – an acronym that has hidden the crucial diversities within a conflated group of people. The longer such acronyms continue circulating, the deeper the challenges faced by invisibilised groups such as transgender people will continue. In this acronym, where and how would we situate the photography of Lebo Ntladi and Jabu Pereira whose lens makes visible queer families or transgender existence? If we do not recognise our individual differences, trans people will remain marginalised and "on their own" even within the LGBT collective, as S'busiso Kheswa argues.

Can we consider the possibilities of earlier existence of gender non-conformity in this continent? What would that look like and how would we understand it now? These are the questions that Unoma Azuah answers when she resurrects and celebrates the late 20th century Nigerian male musician and cross-dresser, Area Scatter. There are not enough images of gender transgressive Africans. This lack of imagery restricts our own thinking and

"

We deliberately use "k" in Afrikan to emphasise the need to reclaim our existence in this continent. As queer persons, we have been alienated in Africa. We have been stripped of our belonging and our connectedness. For these reasons, we have created our own version of Afrika.

language of what we see as gender non-conformity. Often what is permissible within and beyond gender structures does not fit neatly into the Anglophone terminologies we use to describe sexuality and gender. The result is a kind of negotiation with what Jacqui Marx considers an "in/visibility". That you can be both seen and unseen in private and public spaces respectively is central to the queer person.

How do we want to be seen and what do we want people to see? This is a subjective and yet political question that Kylie Thomas raises in relation to some of the photography in this book. Queer persons in this text force you to engage with the way in which we look. To whom does the gaze belong? Is it for the viewer or the viewed? Repositioning the queer body as both the viewer and the viewed is an important stance that alters the way we see. This kind of viewing forces you into an uncomfortable space of seeing yourself as the viewer – thus challenging the ways in which you see.

Perhaps the place where this comes alive most powerfully is in the pieces by both Neo Musangi and a response from Mphati Mutloane and Christopher Ouma. In "In Time and Space" Musangi positions a conversation within the body, with spaces of belonging and with what boundaries and borders permit and restrict. Mutloane and Ouma's reflection on the performance by Musangi in a public space in Nairobi brings us to questions on time-boundedness and notions of "events". Big events have taken place recently in the continent and these are sometimes diffcult to understand. The widely-celebrated public coming out of Kenyan-Ugandan writer Binyavanga Wainaina has stood in stark contrast to the unconsented outing of lesbian, gay and transgender people in Uganda by a tabloid newspaper.

This book is a collaborative curatorial project. In putting all the voices together we have carefully considered space and place. Some of us here exist in academic spaces. Others engage with wider publics as activists and as artists. We are part of families, communities and societies that allow our beings and who are sometimes troubled by our existence. At times our locations and positionalities co-exist. Other times we are troubled by our own sense of being. This is what we are erupting.

The artwork, which is part of this book, is from the exhibition *Critically Queer*, curated by Jabu

Pereira. The title of the exhibition is drawn from Judith Butler's 1993 essay "Critically Queer", in which Butler argues that "[Queer] will have to remain that which is, in the present, never fully owned" (19). The idea that galleries and exhibitions can display visual narratives of a non-normative nature, is in itself a subversive curatorial approach. This exhibition is not so much about displaying artworks, but rather it becomes a convergence of discomforts pertaining to the white cube, which originates within colonial history and criminalised laws on sexuality, which too originate within a colonial legal framework. Hence, Critically Queer reclaims Afrika and a full embodiment of sex, sexuality, erotics, utopia and the continued struggle against oppression.

Jack Halberstam in this book argues for queer work and scholarship that speaks outside the predominant white American or European discourse. Halberstam, following others, calls for queers of colour to claim space, both in Africa and globally. In South Africa specifically, Halberstam argues that through projects such as the Critically Queer exhibition "a deep archive of queer visual culture in Africa today" about Black queerness has emerged.

From the different corners of Africa, artists have come together to reimagine the world they (desire to) live in. Nigeria's Tyna Adebowale offers her complex dual identities. Can Nigeria be comfortable seeing Tyna as both feminine and masculine, male and female? Would there be a time in Kenya when people see Neo Musangi's body as a reflection of the hybridity that underlies the Kenyan existence? How are we to make sense of Dineo Bopape's video installations light switch and state of emergency? Bopape entitles these videos specifically to resurface the issues of being seen and the state in which queer persons find themselves. We live in an "urgent" moment – the responses to the events that happen to queer persons require a certain urgency.

Selogadi Mampane opens the exhibition Critically Queer with Chromotherapy, a performance following a young, queer artist who undergoes the process of constructing their identity. Mampane asks us to be face to face with the violence that is perpetrated on the Black African female body, giving reference to histories of exoticisation and hypersexualising of the Black woman. What does it mean for Black African queer persons to claim their own identity? This is similar to what Kelobogile

(Lebo) Ntladi frames in photography on transgender and androgynous persons. Can we find a space in this world for queer persons to bridge the distances between their bodies and the societies they live in?

Milumbe Haimbe's graphic novel, The Revolutionist, set in the near future takes us to the space of the imaginary, a future whose sexuality, attraction and bodily desire go beyond same-sex attraction. Haimbe's protagonist in the novel posits her object of desire as a robot amidst futuristic Black female superheroes. Hers is a project that offers futuristic visions that are full of life and hope. This makes us wonder and question – is Africa ready? Can we imagine a world where consenting sexuality is not heavily policed? What futures are available to us as Africans?

Various other people and organisations have been resourceful in putting this collaborative curatorial project together. The Iranti-org team in Johannesburg has mobilised, fund-raised and organised different aspects of this project. We acknowledge Meghna Singh's assistance in putting the exhibition together at the Centre for African Studies Gallery. Hivos offered a small grant to put this book together and we thank them for giving us freedom to do exactly what we want. Colleen Higgs at Modjaji Books embraced this book wholeheartedly and has been willing to accommodate the ideas that we envisioned. She has been an ideal publisher for this kind of book. We also thank Karen Jennings as well as the peer reviewers who read the text with open minds.

This entire project would not have been possible without the full support and funding from Huma (Institute for Humanities in Africa) at the University of Cape Town through the Vice Chancellor's Strategic Fund. We also want to acknowledge colleagues at Huma: Deborah Posel, Ilana van Wyk, Rifqah Kahn, Heather Maytham, Shamil Jeppie and the doctoral fellows, for their support and assistance in collaborating in the entire project.

Zethu Matebeni & Jabu Pereira

REFERENCE

Butler, Judith. "Critically Queer." GLQ: A Journal of Lesbian and Gay Studies 1 (1993): 17–32. Print.

KELEBOGILE NTLADI

*T*hebeautifulonesarehere is a photo essay. A collage of different environments in the city, made from photographs to create a collage.

The aim is to use various visual arts, in this case photography and collage, and start building or creating spaces that liberate gender. Neither male nor female, neither particularly masculine nor feminine, where the body and biology do not exist. The only thing that exists is identity, allowing any identity to exist. So the intention is to imply the body and create hybrids, human/mythical/animal traits with urban culture and geometric/technological enhancements. These enhancements will consistently be in a gold-like or metallic colour. The gold places emphasis on the reclaiming of wealth, minerals and land and identity for black people. The mythical/animal hybrid speaks of an earlier, child-like spirit, where anything is possible.

These works call for optimistic, creative and assertive ways in which to eliminate gender pronouns and gender normativity. It calls for unique ways of celebrating indifference and creating cultures and traditions that do not confine or repress but instead cultivate the imaginations of children and child-like spirits to create colourful and positive social change in Africa.

Thebeautifulonesarehere, 2014 ▶

Kelebogile Ntladi

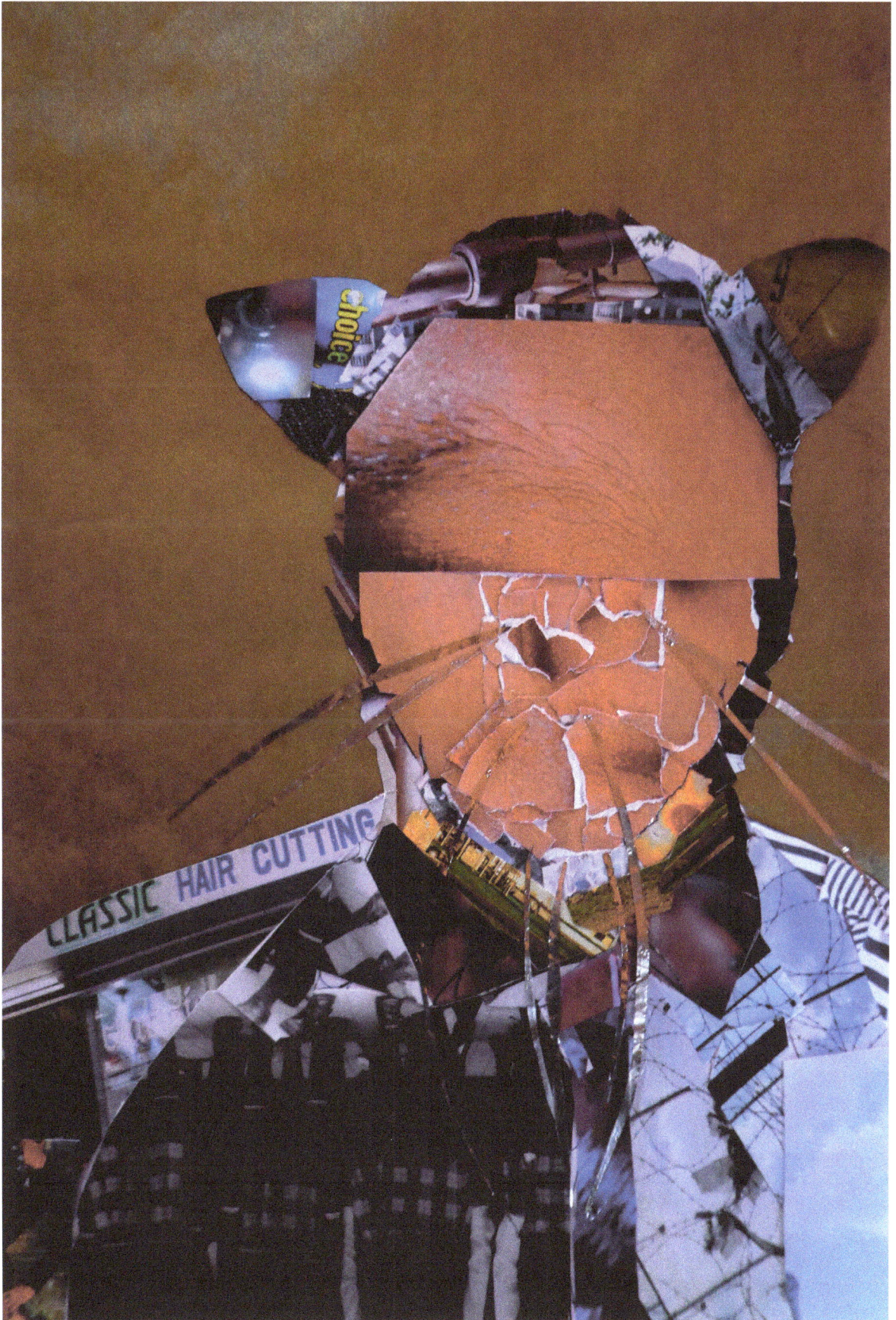

INTRODUCTION

While the fantasies, aspirations and trajectories of queer politics grind sadly and slowly to a halt in the US and Europe, stalled by the mediocre and complacent politics of marriage and the neo-liberal desire for inclusion, the stakes in queer politics and queer aesthetics become critically important in other sites, for other groups with wilder and more ambitious political goals. And so, we might look, for example, to South Africa and to a human rights queer visual media collective housed in Johannesburg called Iranti-org for a glimmer of what might still be critical and meaningfully resistant about queerness now. And what is critical about queerness now for a Black visual media collective in Johannesburg should in no way be understood simply as a version of what was meant by queerness in the US or Europe in earlier moments. The criticality of queerness in the context of Black South Africa, indeed, depends absolutely upon its refutation of a temporality that places Euro-American sexual politics in the center of modernity; and it locates queerness, here and now, as simultaneously a postcolonial critique of normative historiographies of queer worlds and a futuristic summons for a new world-making endeavour that joins queer of colour critique in the US to critical queerness in South Africa.

If we wanted to find links between queer material on radical politics in the US and queer discourse elsewhere, we would do well to start with material on race and sexuality under the heading of "queer of colour critique." It is this strand of queer theory, a strand authored by theorists like Roderick Ferguson, Chandan Reddy, José E. Muñoz, Martin Manalansan and Fatima El Tayeb that speaks most clearly to non-US-centric work and to the alternate time frames and different political trajectories that characterise much of the queer impetus outside of a Euro-American context. For example, the work of Fatima El Tayeb creates one potential bridge between the concerns of queers of colour in the US and Europe and political aspirations among other global queer groups.

El-Tayeb's work is important because it addresses the racism that lies at the very heart of US and European understandings of the nation. In her outstanding book, *European Others: Queering Ethnicity in Postnational Europe* (2011), Tayeb explains how and why European queers of colour have articulated a potent and durable critique of European racism. While white Europeans persist in believing that such traditions of racism were eradicated by benevolent and humanitarian anti-genocidal politics in the wake of the Holocaust, El-Tayeb shows exactly how white supremacy lives on in anti-immigrant policies in contemporary Europe and especially in Germany. Reaching back to the late 19th century for her evidence, El-Tayeb addresses the historical conditions that have produced Black Europeans, and specifically Black Germans as a seeming impossibility within modern Europe. The production of the German state as white has a history that, as in other European nations, overlapped with imperial ambitions, colonial expansion and 19th century theories of race and difference. As El-Tayeb argues convincingly in an article on "Colonialism and Citizenship in Modern Germany", historians have tended to see Anti-Semitism as the only form that racism has taken in Germany and the role of racism directed at other ethnic minorities has been downplayed. Accordingly, the long history of racialist thinking in Germany that targeted Black Africans and others as primitive and inferior gives way to histories of the transformation of 19th century Anti-Semitism into genocidal 20th century versions. But El-Tayeb demonstrates the importance of thinking Anti-Semitism and other forms of German anti-Black racism *together* and cites examples from German colonial history of the deployment of genocidal logics of extermination and elimination used against Black Africans before they became the centerpiece of mid-twentieth century Anti-Semitic policies. German colonialists also advocated against racial mixing on the grounds that the "superior" white races would be polluted and would decline in

Split Halves, 2012 ▲

Lebo Ntladi

power and purity if they intermarried with "inferior" races. The absence of histories such as the one El-Tayeb traces of the 1905 ban on interracial marriages in German Southwest Africa obscures the discursive architecture that still constructs contemporary German citizenship as white and produces Blackness as a primary marker of the foreign and inassimilable.

Some of the most powerful sections of *European Others: Queering Ethnicity* are devoted to accounts of queer of colour activist groups and their organised opposition, activist and aesthetic, to neo-nationalist assaults on immigrant populations. In her meditations on groups like *Kanak Attak* in Berlin and *Strange Fruit* in Amsterdam, El-Tayeb takes the critique of European neo-racisms to a new level and she shapes a coherent set of political aims and practices out of what are often cast as disparate, disorganised and wholly separate groups. In these

detailed and theoretical accounts of the work of queer of colour activist groups, El-Tayeb opens up an archive through which to think translocally about similar groups around the globe – groups like the Sylvia Rivera Transgender Legal Project in NYC, but also Iranti in Johannesburg. These groups share many features and can be read together as part of a global effort to critique state-authored racism from a wide range of subject positions which, in their resistance to discrete identifications, can productively be labelled "queer of colour".

We might also use El-Tayeb's theoretical architecture to frame the continuing legacies of apartheid in contemporary South Africa or continuing

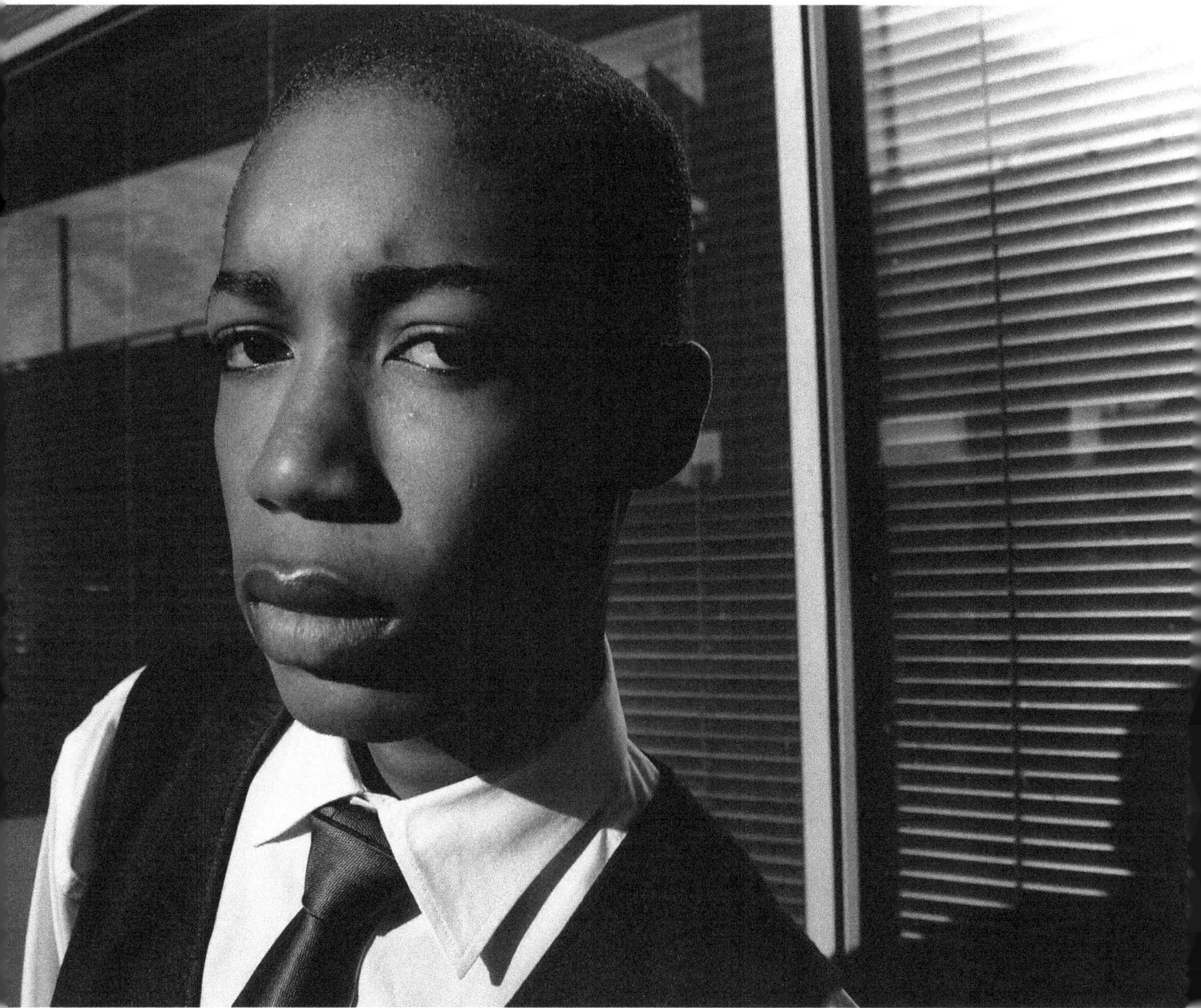

▲ *Split Halves*, 2012

Kelebogile Ntladi

> **Many critics in the art world are content to learn about one or two South African Black artists, few people outside of South Africa know much about entire communities of Black queer artists from the African continent. European curators ignore the deep archive of queer visual culture in Africa today.**

brutal legacies of colonialism in contemporary Africa in general. By showing how and where queer of colour activist groups are able to poke holes in neo-liberal fantasies of democratic freedom and equality, El-Tayeb makes queer of colour activism completely central to contemporary radical anti-nationalist and anti-neo-colonial projects.

And so we can turn to the exhibit labelled *Critically Queer* and hosted by Huma (the Institute for Humanities in Africa) and the University of Cape Town to think about the queer critique of racism as it plays out in Black queer art and visual media collectives in South Africa and other parts of Africa. While many critics in the art world are content to learn about one or two South African Black artists at a time, few people outside of South Africa know much about entire communities of Black queer artists from the African continent. The work that makes it out of Africa and into European art shows is often the tip of the iceberg and allows curators to ignore the deep archive of queer visual culture in Africa today.

Critically Queer challenges stereotypes of African gays and lesbians and makes visible the wide array of art and visual culture currently being produced in South Africa by Black gays, lesbians and trans people. Photographs by Kelebogile Ntladi under the title *Split Halves* and the photo essay *thebeautifulonesarehere*, for example, capture the fragmentations of self that result from the violent history of South Africa, a history that plays itself out through and across Black queer bodies in ways that are exceedingly hard to capture in anything like conventional portraiture. These images in *Split Halves* remind the viewer of the damage done, and being done, to Black bodies—

sometimes by white brutality sometimes by other Black bodies—on a daily basis.

The body in Ntladi's striking images falls into shadow more often than not and is cut through by architectures, blinds, the shutter itself. Ntladi, indeed, constructs Blackness as literally a visage moving in and out of focus, neither seeking clarity nor resigned to the blurred lines of amorphous being. Ntladi's images liken the experience of Black transgender embodiment to an inability to capture identity within the frame of the visual and they simultaneously betray a deep distrust of the mechanics of visual culture.

Startling work by the queer Zambian artist Milumbe Haimbe turns away from the lingering wounds of the past and imagines the coming violence of the future. In a stunning graphic novel titled *The Revolutionist*, Haimbe tells the story of a near future society in which women are being replaced by robots. An underground resistance group named Army for the Restoration of Womanhood sends someone to infiltrate the corporation and destroy the robots... But along the way, the infiltrator falls for the robot and chaos ensues! It is an awesome story and Haimbe tells it using cool digital graphics. Her futuristic Black feminist superheroes are flawed and powerful, sexy and serious and the whole book oozes charisma and teems with utopian and dystopian potential.

This futuristic vision reminds us of how thoroughly the past and the future are being remade by and within activist groups of colour on the African continent. Taking aim simultaneously at the legacies of racism that continue to thwart political progress and the contemporary manifestations of homophobia that make day to day life precarious for queers of colour, *Critically Queer* as a show points the way to radically new articulations of sexuality, race and postcolonial political futures. And Iranti, the visual activist group out of which this show and many more activist projects emerged, offers a brilliant example of the radical queer of colour activism that El-Tayeb situates at the very heart of post-nationalist queer community.

Jack Halberstam

REFERENCES
El Tayeb, Fatima. *European Others. Queering Ethnicity in Postnational Europe*. University of Minnesota Press, 2011. Print

MILUMBE HAIMBE

The Revolutionist' is set in the near future that is dominated by a corporation. Social conformity in the interest of the collective is subliminally reinforced through symbolism and iconology, while the economy is purely corporate-driven. Exploitation of human by human thrives and the insatiable appetite for sex robots threatens to tip the already delicate social balance. But the turning point arrives when news spreads that the corporation is developing a prototype robot that is so sophisticated that it is capable of replacing women. This gives rise to the resistance. Calling itself the "Army for the Restoration of Womanhood", its tactics include espionage and information dissemination. Ananiya was only 13 years old when she joined the resistance. Now at 17 she has recently been appointed as an agent in the Covert Operations Division. In the ensuing standoff where the corporation increasingly maintains control with an ironclad fist, it is not long before the resistance galvanizes into a full-blown revolution. As the masses are thrust into a state of emergency characterised by curfews, police raids, censorship and propaganda, Ananiya emerges as the most unlikely hero for the revolution. But not only does she have to contend with a cold war whose underbelly is often dark and ugly, but she must also survive the perils and growing pains of being a teenager, as well as human. Will the revolution overcome?

A GIANT CORPORATION RUNS THE WORLD. RESOURCES ARE PLENTY BUT IT GRASPS 95% OF THIS COMMON WEALTH IN IT'S STEELY GRIP.

THREE EMPERORS SIT AT THE TOP OF THE TOWER, TURNING GIANT WHEELS.

A SYSTEM WHERE THE WORTH OF A WOMAN IS MEASURED IN A UNIT POUND OF FLESH.

THEIR REACH IS SO GREAT THAT SOON POWER, GREED AND LUST BECOME THE SYSTEM BY WHICH THE POWERLESS BECOME MORE POWERLESS.

ONE
CONSCIOUSNESS
CORPORATION

ONE

BUT NOT EVEN NATURE COULD FORGE THE KIND OF BEAUTY THAT THESE MEN DESIRED SO THEY TURNED TO SCIENCE TO CREATE THE PERFECT WOMAN.

THE FIRST GENERATION OF ROBOTS WAS CONCEIVED TO THE SATISFACTION OF THEIR DESIRES.

BY GENERATION 5, THE CORPORATION ENACTED A LAW THAT ENABLED HUMANS TO MARRY ROBOTS.

IN THIS NEW WORLD ORDER WOMEN WERE DEEMED TO BE OBSOLETE.

SOME DISSIDENTS GALVANISED INTO THE RESISTANCE, CALLING THEMSELVES **ARMY FOR THE RESTORATION OF WOMANHOOD.**

THEIR AGENDA WAS TO CHALLENGE THE VERY EXISTENCE OF THE ROBOTS. TACTICS INCLUDED ESPIONAGE AND INFORMATION DISSEMINATION.

ANANIYA WAS ONLY 13 YEARS OLD WHEN SHE JOINED THE RESISTANCE.

SUBCITY ARACHNIDA, RESISTANCE HEADQUARTERS:

NOW AT 17, SHE HAS RECENTLY BEEN APPOINTED AS AN AGENT IN THE **COVERT OPERATIONS DIVISION.**

HEY ARUSHA, WHAT'S UP?

THIS COULD TAKE A WHILE. WHY DON'T YOU SIT DOWN?

HOW DO YOU FEEL ABOUT GOING ON YOUR FIRST ASSIGNMENT AS COVERT AGENT?

I'M COOL. YOU'RE THE LEADER. ASSIGN AWAY.

WE HAVE JUST RECEIVED INFORMATION THAT THE CORPORATION IS DEVELOPING A GENERATION 8 PROTOTYPE ROBOT. ACCORDING TO THE INFORMANT...

THE PROTOTYPE'S SO SOPHISTICATED THAT YOU CAN'T TELL IT APART FROM THE REAL THING. IT'S EVEN BEEN GENERICALLY NAMED **FREJA.**

WE'VE GOT TO STOP THIS MODEL FROM GOING INTO MASS-PRODUCTION. THAT MEANS SABOTAGING THE WHOLE OPERATION BEFORE THE PROTOTYPE'S COMPLETE.

YOUR MISSION, CODE-NAMED **OPERATION FREJA**, IS TO INFILTRATE THE CORPORATION'S ROBOTICS PLANT.

OUR INSIDER HAS ALREADY CREATED THE PERFECT COVER FOR YOU - INTERN, DESIGN UNIT..

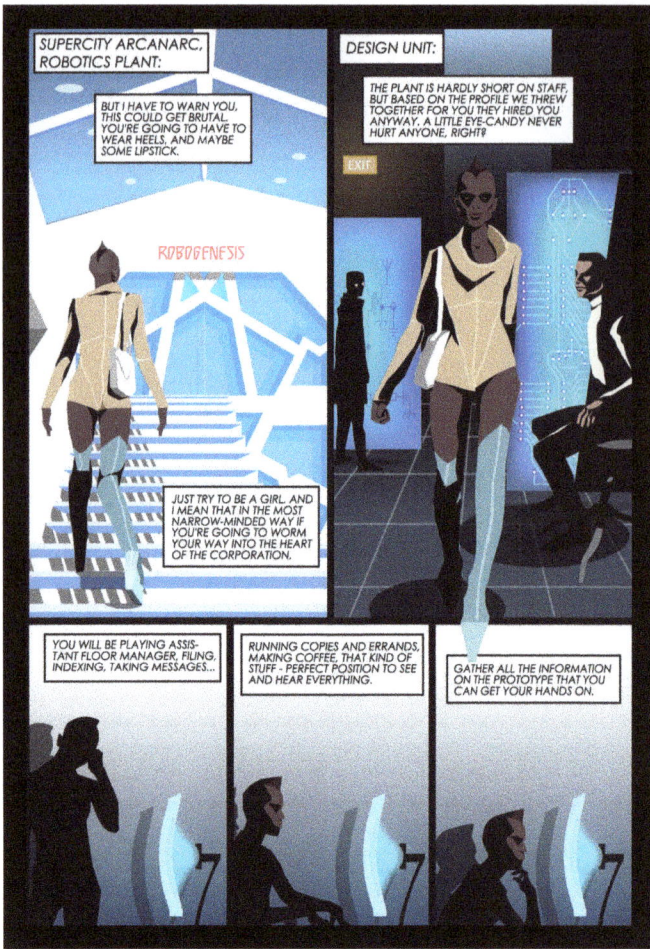

SUPERCITY ARCANARC, ROBOTICS PLANT:

BUT I HAVE TO WARN YOU, THIS COULD GET BRUTAL. YOU'RE GOING TO HAVE TO WEAR HEELS, AND MAYBE SOME LIPSTICK.

ROBOGENESIS

JUST TRY TO BE A GIRL. AND I MEAN THAT IN THE MOST NARROW-MINDED WAY IF YOU'RE GOING TO WORM YOUR WAY INTO THE HEART OF THE CORPORATION.

DESIGN UNIT:

THE PLANT IS HARDLY SHORT ON STAFF, BUT BASED ON THE PROFILE WE THREW TOGETHER FOR YOU THEY HIRED YOU ANYWAY. A LITTLE EYE-CANDY NEVER HURT ANYONE, RIGHT?

EXIT

YOU WILL BE PLAYING ASSISTANT FLOOR MANAGER, FILING, INDEXING, TAKING MESSAGES...

RUNNING COPIES AND ERRANDS, MAKING COFFEE, THAT KIND OF STUFF - PERFECT POSITION TO SEE AND HEAR EVERYTHING.

GATHER ALL THE INFORMATION ON THE PROTOTYPE THAT YOU CAN GET YOUR HANDS ON.

WE NEED YOU TO FIGURE OUT THE SCHEMATICS OF THE PRODUCTION LINE AND THE LAYOUT OF THE PLANT IN GENERAL

LABORATORY

FIND THE WEAK SPOTS AND ENTRY POINTS, AND DON'T PASS UP ANY CHANCE TO DOCUMENT EVERY SINGLE DETAIL, AND ANANIYA, BE VERY CAREFUL!

NEED I REMIND YOU THAT THE CORPORATION IS VIRTUALLY OMNIPOTENT?

THOSE STATS WERE OFF THE CHART. LOOKS LIKE WE MIGHT HAVE TO SHUT DOWN THE PROTOTYPE...

LABORATORY

A NEURAL MUTATION IN THE COGNITIVE PROCESSOR CAUSED THE FAULT. CAN'T WE FIX IT?

AND RESTART THE PROJECT FROM SCRATCH.

THE MUTATION IS NON-GENERIC. IT WILL COST US A LOT MORE TO FIX IT THAN TO TAKE THE PROJECT BACK TO THE DRAWING BOARD.

AND EVEN THEN, IT'S A RISK I'M NOT WILLING TO TAKE IN CASE THE ALGORITHMS DON'T ADD UP AT MASS-PRODUCTION LEVEL

ON ACCOUNT OF BINARY RANDOMS AND OTHER UNFORESEEABLE VARIABLES.

LABORATORY

I GET IT. IT'S A GLITCH IN THE WIRING IN OUR LITTLE WORLD,

BUT OUT THERE IN THE BIG BAD WORLD IT'S AN INQUISITION WAITING TO HAPPEN.

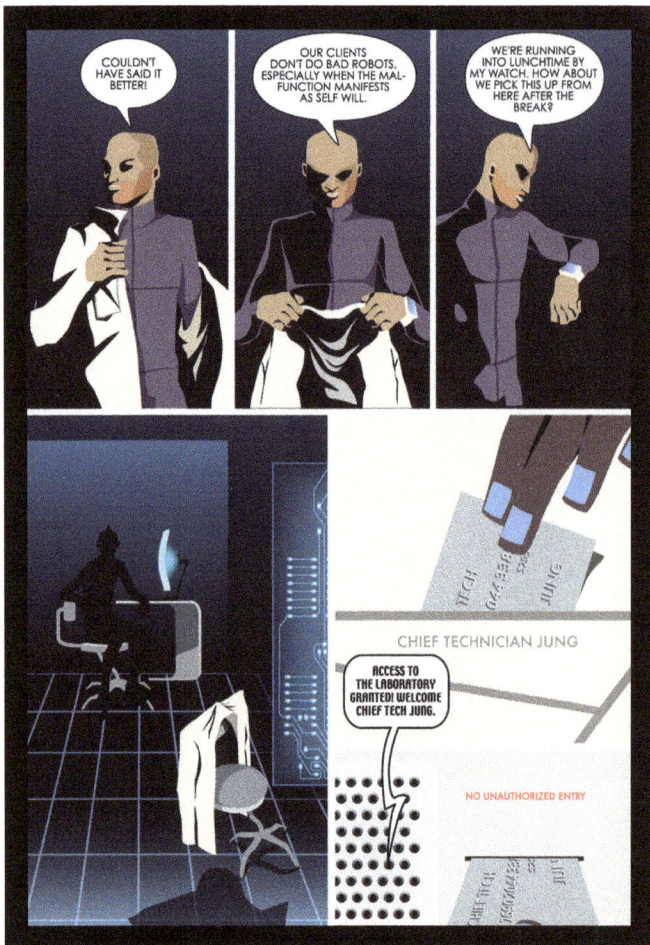

COULDN'T HAVE SAID IT BETTER!

OUR CLIENTS DON'T DO BAD ROBOTS, ESPECIALLY WHEN THE MALFUNCTION MANIFESTS AS SELF WILL.

WE'RE RUNNING INTO LUNCHTIME BY MY WATCH. HOW ABOUT WE PICK THIS UP FROM HERE AFTER THE BREAK?

TECH 004.5.5218.520

JUNG

CHIEF TECHNICIAN JUNG

ACCESS TO THE LABORATORY GRANTED! WELCOME CHIEF TECH JUNG.

NO UNAUTHORIZED ENTRY

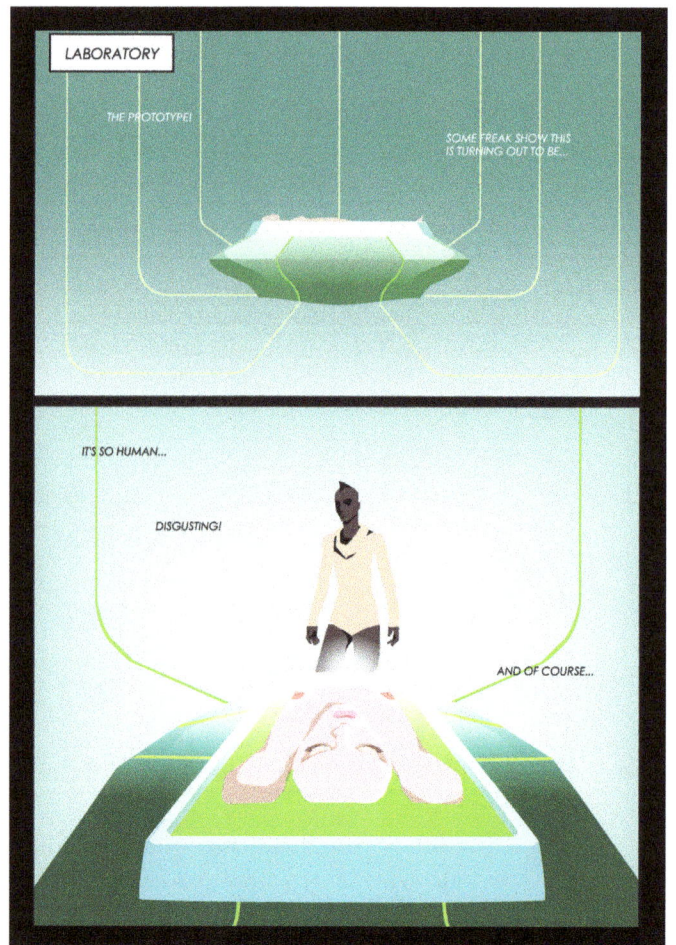

LABORATORY

THE PROTOTYPE!

SOME FREAK SHOW THIS IS TURNING OUT TO BE...

IT'S SO HUMAN...

DISGUSTING!

AND OF COURSE...

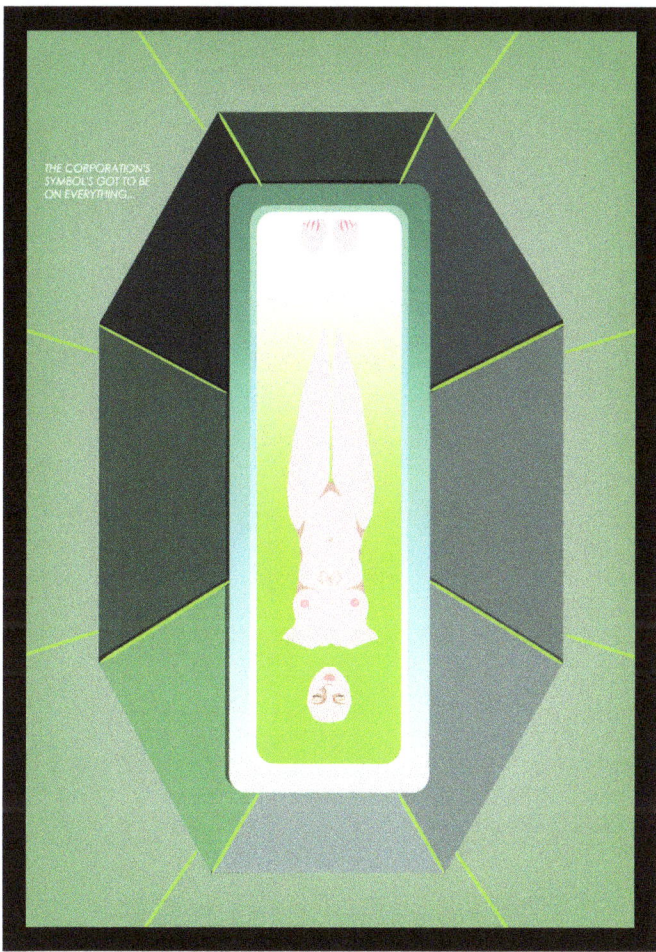

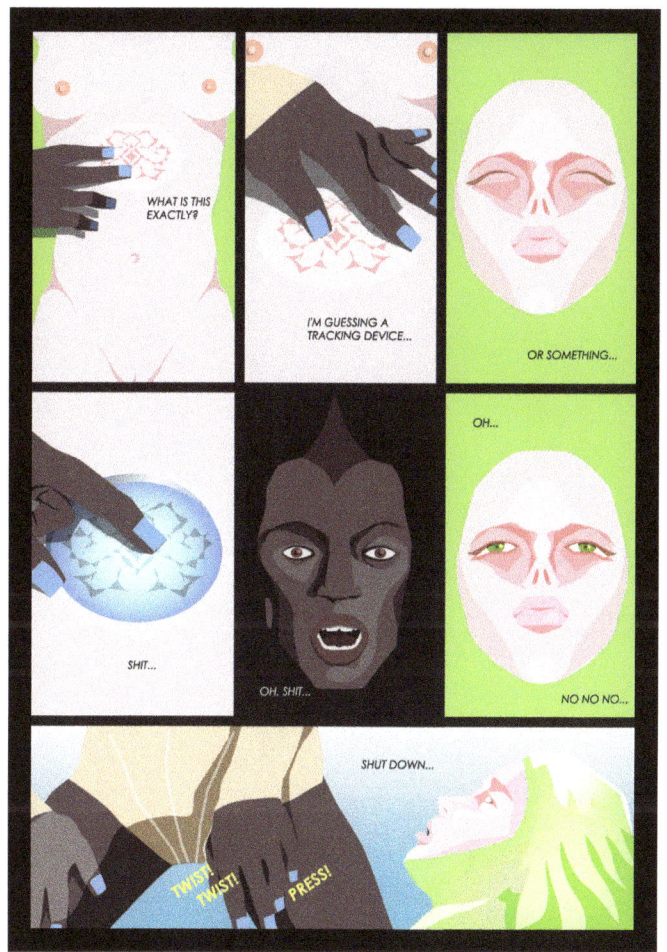

RESURRECTING AND CELEBRATING AREA SCATTER,

A CROSS-DRESSER WHO TRANSGRESSED GENDER NORMS IN EASTERN NIGERIA

by **Unoma Azuah**

This essay examines the role of patriarchy in Nigeria's societal opposition to homosexuality; the challenge to that opposition by the late Area Scatter, a renowned late 20th century Nigerian male musician and cross-dresser; and Scatter's personification of ideas stemming from the framework of Queer Theory.

For centuries, the Nigerian political, religious, and social order has been dictated by a patriarchal system that puts in place fixed gender roles and attitudes opposing homosexuality. Along with foreign religions and colonialism, patriarchy is the cause to which many historians attribute homophobia in African countries. Professor Mark Epprecht of Queens University in Canada, for example, notes that homophobic laws entrenched in colonised countries were inherited from the colonial era and are, in large part, responsible for hostility toward homosexuality in Nigeria. This fact is evident when looking at the pre-colonial era of the Igbo community in southeastern Nigeria. During that period of Igbo history, sex and gender were fluid, and even though there were societies in Nigeria that were not open to transgendered persons, there were/are instances where men cross-dress, as in the Gelede Yoruba festival where men cross-dress to honour motherhood as Margaret Drewal documents.

Further, sociologist Chimaroke O. Izugbara argues that norms around sexuality in Nigeria "are socially produced and fed by oppressive patriarchal subjectivities and ideologies that try to instill a sense of what is normal, sexually-speaking, for us all" (12). Homosexuality is one of the strongest challenges to patriarchy, and therefore "is framed as an unruly force which threatens humanity at large and has to be kept perfectly under control, by violence, if necessary" (12). While different strategies are used to control homosexuality, all of them including religious, and governmental, reinforce patriarchal power.

The cross-dressing musical performer, Area Scatter was defiant of patriarchal tradition. It is believed that in the year 1970 Scatter retreated to a vast and secluded wooded area for seven months and seven days after which he re-emerged transformed. Some of the speculations attached to his transformation point to the spiritual implication of his seclusion which says that during the period he acquired spiritual powers to enhance his musical talent. Some others suggest that he needed the seclusion to fortify himself as a man who needed to embrace his femininity. In *Beats of the Heart* (1985), where Scatter is featured alongside important but lesser-known international musicians, researchers give the following account:

◀ *Identity Series #4, 2014*

Tyna Adebowale

We headed off into the forests to the hut of an infamous "witch doctor", or shaman, called Area Scatter. His home was filled with bones and skulls and paintings of the power of good and evil. A muscular, humorous man, he explained how, after living through the civil war, he had gone into the wilderness for seven months and seven days and had reappeared transformed into a woman. The day we visited him he headed off, dressed in white smock, polka-dot skirt and a shamanist bone necklace, to the residence of his Royal Highness… to play for the local king and queen. Area Scatter was a highly accomplished performer on his thumb piano which was decorated with distinctive skull and crossbones. When the king and his wife ceremonially entered and seated themselves on their thrones, Area Scatter bowed deeply and started to sing in a soft, rich voice.

Area Scatter's performance, seen on a YouTube video, at the palace of a local chief creates queer moments, undoing the culturally sanctioned gender norm as the men in the audience react to him with fascination and, perhaps, desire.

The response to his exhibition of trans-status and transgender symbolises and magnifies the hypocrisy and blurred boundaries of sexuality in the larger society. The chief for whom Area Scatter performed was receptive to and seemingly enamored with the performance of the cross-dresser. However, the chief represents the society's patriarchal power structure that enacts laws forbidding homosexuality and punishing it with jail and death sentences. Sections 214 and 217 of the Nigeria Criminal Code states that adults who engage in consensual same sex activities will be penalised with a jail sentence of up to 14 years. Section 217 also criminalises an even broader category of "gross indecency" between males, punishing the offender with up to three years in prison. This is because homosexual men in Nigeria more publicly transgress gender norms, especially with the belief that men should be dominant over submissive women. By rejecting the privilege enjoyed by heterosexual men, homosexual men represent a visible threat to

Flipped Side Series, 2014 ▲

Tyna Adebowale

patriarchal values and the sexual ideologies they support. The Sharia Penal Code stipulates the severest of punishment for same-sex relations – a maximum penalty of death by stoning. Further, the Same Sex Marriage (Prohibition) Act of 2014 has introduced a law that sentences any convicted homosexual who engages in same sex marriage or civil union to a 14 year jail term. These policies reflect the profuse homophobia and homohatred of the Nigerian government.

Within the performance space of Area Scatter and his audience, the cross-dressing entertainer shatters the generally accepted interpretations of gender and sexuality in

Area Scatter's performance at the palace of a local chief creates queer moments, undoing the culturally sanctioned gender norm as the men in the audience react to him with fascination and, perhaps, desire.

Area Scatter's intent when she says that "the conscious act of cross dressing ... is a thought out and active attempt to subvert gender identity" (n. pag.). Additionally, Queer Theorists like Bertens, and Hans have said that, "Cross-dressing undermines the claim to the naturalness of standard heterosexual identities. Therefore cross-dressing acts as a hefty weapon in the battle against the fixed categorization of the phallocentric center" (230). In this context, one can say that Area Scatter takes the role of a homosexual because he utilises homosexuality to defy fixed gender constructs and expectations. Hence, he dismantles gender boundaries.

From a larger perspective, his performance calls to mind the act of cross-dressing in medieval plays. This period may seem dated, but it evokes issues of queer moments that are relevant to modern times. These stage actors in their customs bear transgender and trans-status demonstrations that move beyond contravening proscribed sexual and social behaviours to introducing multiple interpretations of desire (Sponsler & Clark 319-344). The parallel between Area Scatter's stage and that of the actors of the late Middle Ages stirs up issues of performance and its social framework. There seems to be a clear message that performance is a mode of conveying intense social and erotic desires. Whatever meaning one reads into Area Scatter's performance, there is a suggestion of some sort, albeit subtle, of an erotic energy from his male audience. Though both Area Scatter and medieval actors use the stage and performance as sites of desire, a point of departure comes between the two, particularly when it is

a community fixated on gender roles and draconian laws created to suppress so-called "deviant" behaviours of the LGBT (Lesbian, Gay, Bisexual, and Transgender) community in Nigeria. He presented himself as a woman not just on stage but in life. This is demonstrated when he is seen walking to a local Chief's palace in his community to perform. His femininity was not merely his garb or costume. He walked the streets of his community as a woman. In other words, his cross dressing is not regalia he dons for his performance. Instead, he owns and embodies a gender that is different from his biological make-up. Hence, he lived his life unconfined to stringent spaces relegated by imposing order, validating the belief that femininity and masculinity are not always behaviours that come from biology. In fact, one can conclude that Karen Melanson aptly captures

> **Area Scatter as a cross dresser defies the notion of a fixed gender and celebrates the fluidity of gender. He transgresses the social, gender and sexual norms of his community and, therefore, should be celebrated for his bravery.**

implied that cross-dressing could be tamed by confining it to spaces of what is called "licensed misrule saturnalia" to use Casey Charles' term (122). Additionally, Jean Howard suggests that crossdressing transgresses status hierarchies and provides a conduit for questioning and in some cases attempts to re-arrange the construction of class as well as gender boundaries (418-440).

In a society like Nigeria where the belief is that men should be dominant over submissive women, homosexual men more publicly transgress gender norms. Yet, Area Scatter as a cross-dresser defies the notion of a fixed gender and celebrates the fluidity of gender. He rather transgresses the social, gender and sexual norms of his community and, therefore, should be celebrated for his bravery. Though he is late, his legacy foreshadows a society where there is no discrimination against sexual orientation. He must have imagined a society where gender is fluid and destabilised, a society where gender becomes irrelevant to the individual's perception and demonstration of self (Melanson). Area Scatter is a Queer theorist of his time because he aligns himself with Judith Butler's assertion that sex is biological while gender is a cultural construction (284).

REFERENCES

Bertens, Johannes Willem and Iertens Hans. *The Basics: Literary Theory.* New York: Routledge Publishers, 2004. Print.

Butler, Judith. *Gender Trouble: Feminism and the Subversion of Identity*. New York: Routledge Classic, 2006. Print.

Charles, Casey. "Gender Trouble in Twelfth Night" *Theatre Journal*. 49.2 (1997): 121-141. Print.

Clark, L.A. and Claire M. Sponster. "Queer Play: The Cultural Work of Cross-dressing in Medieval Drama." *New Literary History*. 28.2 (1997): 319-44. Print.

Drewal, Margaret Thompson. "Art and Trance among Yoruba Shango Devotees." *Africa Art*. 20. (1986): 60-99. Print.

Epprecht, Marc. *Heterosexuality Africa? The History of an idea from the Age of Exploration to the Age of AIDS*. Ohio: Ohio University Press, 2008. Print.

Izugbara, Chimaroke O. "Patriarchal Ideology and Discourses of Sexuality in Nigeria." *Understanding Human Sexuality Seminar Series 2*. Lagos, Nigeria: Africa Regional Sexuality Resources Center, 2004. Print.

Howard, Jean E. "Crossdressing, The Theatre, and Gender Struggle in Early Modern England." *Shakespeare Quarterly* 39 (1988): 418-440. Print.

Melanson, Karen. "Queer Theory: Destabilizing Gender." *Femtheory*. Tulane University. 2013. Web.

Area Scatter video clip https://www.youtube.com/watch?v=X8DYlDQh20Q

◄ *Shy*, 2012

Tyna Adebowale

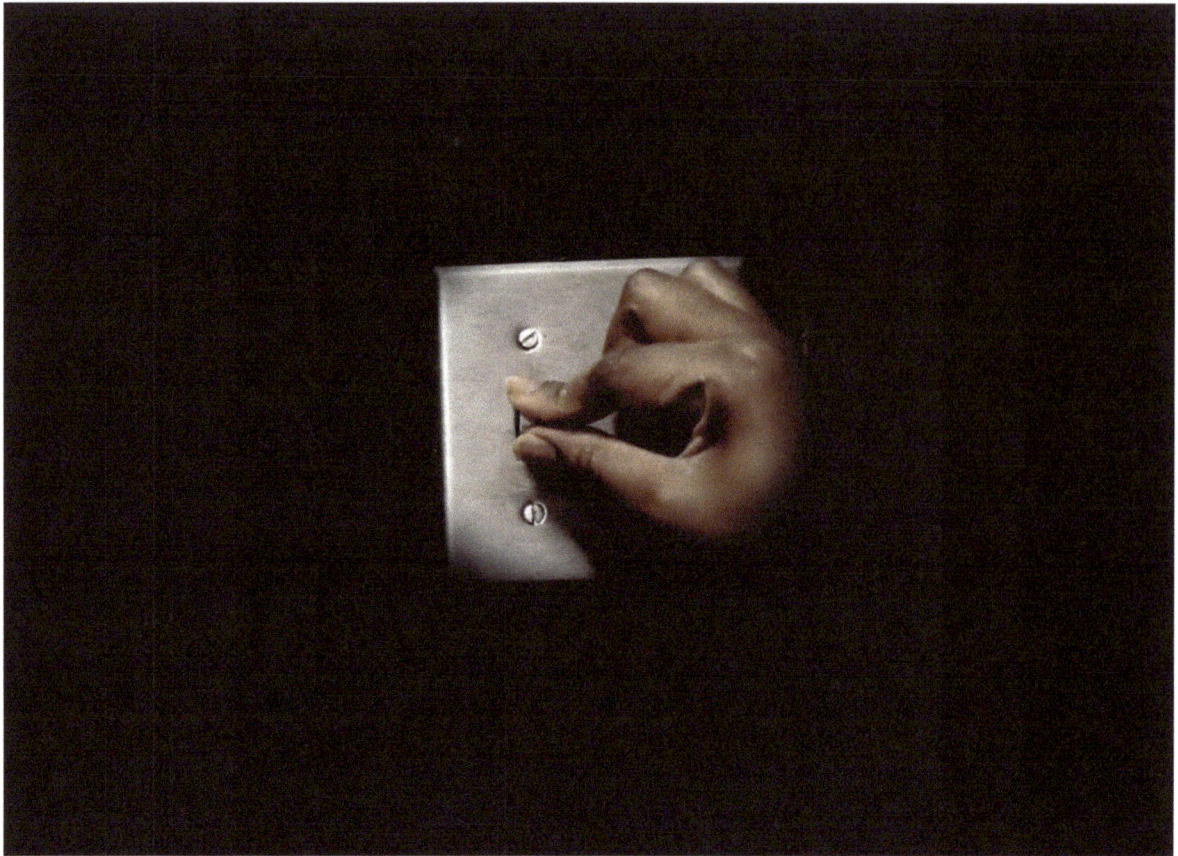

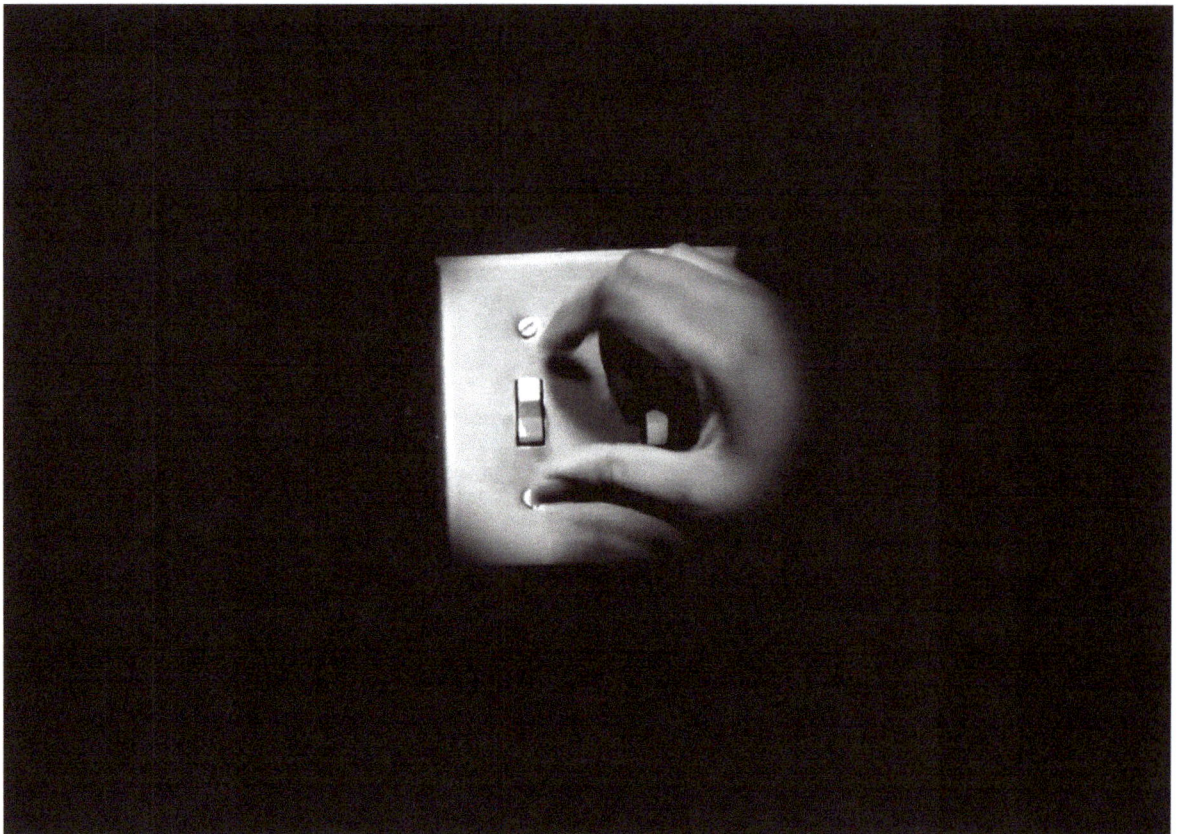

NEGOTIATING HOMOSEXUAL IN/VISIBILITY

by **Jacqueline Marx**

In the exhibition *Critically Queer*, Dineo Seshee Bopape presents a looped projection in which two light switches are turned on and off. The viewer experiences seeing and not seeing, which symbolizes a dimension of homosexual existence: in/visibility. As sexuality is not immediately obvious in the way that gender and race is (its perceptibility is more contingent on our performance of it), it is interesting to consider the circumstances in which homosexual in/visibility is negotiated. In this essay, this consideration is grounded in a discussion of cross-dressing and drag performances in a small city in the Eastern Cape Province of South Africa.

This essay is based on stories about cross-dressing and drag performances that were obtained from personal interviews. Although this essay focuses on the politics of homosexual in/visibility in post-apartheid South Africa, it is based on doctoral research that investigates the politics of homosexual in/visibility over a period of sixty years, beginning in the 1950s and the inception of apartheid policy, through the socio-political changes in the 1990s, to the twenty-first century post-apartheid context. An excerpt from a conversation with an elderly homosexual man about cross-dressing during apartheid is included in this essay because it allows for a useful observation of shifts in

◀ *Lightswitch*

Dineo Bopape

the exercise of power and the implications of this for homosexual in/visibility in the post-apartheid context.

The prohibition of homosexuality in the apartheid era presented a challenge to its visibility because behaviour that was prohibited by the state could not be seen to occur. However, despite the prohibition of homosexuality and the state mechanisms in place to police the prohibition, practices such as cross-dressing and drag which made homosexuality visible did still occur. The extract below is taken from a conversion with Edward, an elderly white gay man. In this extract Edward describes a scene at a party that he attended in the 1950s, soon after the inception of apartheid policy.

Edward It was in the late 1950s and it was the first drag party that I went to. I remember John turned up in a school gym. The Belles of St Trinian's was showing at the movies and John was in a rather short gym, with black stockings. And ah, I scared the hell out of these people. Because I knew I had to dress-up in some way or other and I had recently discovered most of my father's army uniform, complete with pith helmet. And this is what I rocked up in. In very long shorts, long Khaki shorts, and this pith helmet. And everybody thought I was the police. The panic!

Historically, cross-dressing or drag has been a common feature of gay male parties. There are different explanations for why this should be the case. One is that cross-dressing is a strategy for articulating homosexuality.

The homosexual man who dresses as a woman takes her place, via symbolic dress codes, in the dyad (male/female) through which hegemonic representations of desire are structured – that is, as an attraction to the opposite sex. But, when appropriated, can also make same-sex desire visible. Judith Butler (1991) argues that making homosexuality visible is a political issue because gay men and lesbian women have, historically, been "threatened by the violence of public erasure" (19).

Edward's description of his arrival at the Palm Springs party also provides a rather funny account of how Edward, who considers himself to be a masculine homosexual man, did not want to dress as a woman and so decided to wear his father's old military uniform instead. That is, to dress-up in masculinity rather than cross-dress in femininity. But, unfortunately, it didn't work. The other party goers thought he was the police and they ran away. This is a funny story but it also allows for an important observation about the experience of threat in the apartheid era. In the 1950s, gay men were afraid of the police.

The next extract is taken from a conversation in 2008. At this time South Africa is led by the African National Party (ANC) under whose rule a new South African constitution has been ratified which prohibits discrimination on the basis of sexual orientation in its Bill of Rights. This conservation was with contestants in a gay beauty pageant competition. In these competitions it is traditional for participants to cross-dress. Lesbian women dress in suits and gay men dress in elaborate evening gowns. In this part of the conversation I asked the men what motivated them to participate in the pageants. Their responses are interesting because they provide insight into contemporary experiences of threat.

Jasmine Ah, it's just hiding away from the real world.

Clare What is the *real* world? The real world.

Jasmine That is a question I also ask myself sometimes. The real world is the cruellest world, outside of this place.

Jacqui What is different about this place?

> ## "
> ## The prohibition of homosexuality in the apartheid era presented a challenge to its visibility because behaviour that was prohibited by the state could not be seen to occur. However, despite the prohibition of homosexuality, practices such as cross-dressing and drag which made homosexuality visible did still occur.

Clare Here we are allowed to express hidden feelings that you're not allowed in general to express, in the world outside.

It is interesting that contemporary gay men should talk about having to keep practices such as cross-dressing, which make homosexuality visible, private – that is, to keep it out of the view of the public because this is the sort of thing that happened in the apartheid era when homosexuality was criminalized. The next extract is taken from another conversation with a gay beauty pageant contestant called Violet. In this extract Violet elaborates on the nature of the threat of being visibly homosexual in public.

Violet It's brave to go out in drag because they will discriminate against you. Straight people. I mean, a lot of people won't tolerate that. So ah, I think it all boils down to a factor of fear, at the end of the day. I mean, you don't want this group of people walking up to you, you know, and shoving you in a coffin. Ja, so. Ah, it's scary. But it depends on you, you know. How you feel. If you want to dress like that then go ahead and dress like that. It's your prerogative. It's still scary though.

It is remarkable that the sense of threat that Violet experiences does not pertain to the police or some other state authority as it did during apartheid, but from ordinary people. So, under apartheid rule relations of power were clearly demarcated in state legislation prohibiting homosexuality and the various state apparatuses that were put in place to police the prohibition. While, in the twenty first century, when these policies and apparatuses are being dismantled, the prohibition of homosexuality is shifting and becoming the purview of socio-cultural norms and expectations rather than state sanctioned legal code. The shift from state sanctioned prohibitions of homosexuality to socio-cultural prohibitions of homosexuality evidences a shift in technologies of power, and a shift toward disciplinary power in particular.

Disciplinary power is not the kind of power that is in the hands of the state or powerful elite. Instead, it is the sort of power that is exercised in everyday encounters that are structured by socio-cultural expectations about doing and appropriate doing; for example, in ideas about what constitutes marriage in African culture. Importantly, visibility is a critical aspect of disciplinary power because it is a mechanism for surveillance and the policing of behaviour. This aspect of disciplinary power is useful for understanding the politics of homosexual in/visibility.

Michel Foucault (1977) argues that power works by making individuals visible so that they can be corrected when they step out of line. Or, so that believing that they are being watched, will regulate themselves. According to Judge Edwin Cameron, in the context of pervasive discrimination and stigmatization, the non-obviousness of homosexuality provides a strong impetus for gay men and lesbian women to closet their orientation from outsiders (450). This is evident in the self-regulation that resonates in conversations with gay men about being visibly homosexual in public. Violet's narrative is a good example of this since Violet equates the decision to be visibly homosexual in public space with the management of risk. As Violet says, "it's your prerogative, it's still scary though."

Reflecting on the issue of self-regulation and homosexual in/visibility, Eve Kosofsky Sedgwick (1990) has argued that the closet is the defining structure of homosexual oppression. Certainly, the prevalence of homophobic violence in South Africa that emerges at the same time as the escalating visibility of homosexuality in debates about same-sex unions and the right of homosexuals to adopt and raise children, provides an explanation for the retreat of drag spectacles which make homosexuality visible, into private enclaves within the urban public realm. While I am cognizant that this retreat has implications for the potential of homosexual visibility to transgress or undermine heteronormativity, it has some advantages. For the gay men that I spoke to, the retreat into more private spaces provided a strategy for them to gain control over the threat associated with being marked as homosexual in public.

REFERENCES

Butler, Judith. "Imitation and Gender Insubordination." *Inside/Out: Lesbian Theories, Gay Theories*. Ed. D. Fuss. New York: Routledge, 1991. 13–32. Print.

Cameron, Edward. "Sexual Orientation and the Constitution: A Test Case for Human Rights." *South African Law Journal* 110 (1993): 450-472. Web.

Foucault, Michel. *Discipline and Punish: The Birth of the Prison*. Trans. R Hurley. London: Penguin Books, 1977. Print.

Kosofsky Sedgwick, Eve. *Epistemology of the Closet*. Berkeley: University of California Press, 1990. Print.

PERFORMING QUEER "IN TIME AND SPACE": A "POLITICS OF THE EVENT"

by **Christopher Ouma and Mphati Mutloane**

Sexuality in Africa has been the subject of debate in various spheres of academic and public engagement. More recently published work, particularly Sylvia Tamale's *African Sexualities: A Reader* (2011) as well as *Queer African Reader* (2013) edited by Sokari Ekine and Hakima Abbas, continue to provide varied intellectual platforms of engagement for academics, activists, artists amongst others. However, what continues to make this debate more visible is what can be referred to as a "politics of the event". This phrase is used by Tom Lundborg (4) to engage with the over-determining political act of encountering an event, and the problematic hierarchical nature of what is included and excluded while reading the event. In other words, and in the framework of this essay, certain events within particular contexts of time and space throw into public engagement debates around Lesbian, Gay, Bisexual, Transgender and Intersex (LGBTI) identities. The fact that these are "events" invokes specific spatio-temporal contexts in which "publics" are constructed or construct themselves to participate, to (de)-liberate on the question of LGBTI existence. What is clear to us is that, in most cases, these events are triggered

◀ "Space and Time", Video Series, 2013

Stills from a performance Neo Musangi and Iranti-org

by instances of violence (in all its permutations), various forms of aggression which human rights scholar Makau Mutua places in the context of "liberalism and the foundational norms of human rights" (453). The question of human rights according to Mutua is complexly layered with varied jurisprudential histories, intellectual traditions and spatio-temporal contexts. What is often understated is the very materiality – the irreducible minimum – the human. It is instances of aggression, phobia and violence that call into question this category of the human. Therefore the materiality of the human, the body, comes into even sharper focus. The invocation of the body *as* human and the "publics" around the event of *being* human are the contextual subject of this short essay, based on Neo Musangi's silent cross-dressing performance in a video installation called *In the Closet*.

The subject of this essay is the connection(s) between the body, clothing, sexual and gender identity and how these are read in the event of Neo's cross-dressing performance. We read the performance enacted in a mediated space of everyday city life while considering the (in)visible and audible audience which constitutes itself as a particular "public" in this event. Neo's performance is read in the context of Stephen Frosh's ideas about "sexual difference", taking into consideration the symbolic and cultural contexts of Neo's performance, while arguing that the performance seeks to invoke an alternative and critical imaginary of queer sexuality and identity through the *public* act of cross-dressing.

Neo's cross-dressing performance in one of the busiest streets in the city of Nairobi in Kenya allows us a critical glimpse into the debate on LGBTI in not only Kenya, but also East Africa and the rest of the continent. In this way, specific events in the past few years in East Africa throw into sharp relief the significance of Neo's performance. It comes in the wake of the anti-homosexuality bill in the Ugandan parliament that has since been passed into law, as well as the 'miniskirt law'. In the background is also Nigeria's anti-same-same marriage law promulgated in January 2014. These legislative "performances" have continued to expose the contradictory nature of a variously layered idea of what it means to be "African". Indeed the very convenient coalitions of nationalist hetero-patriarchies across Ugandan, Nigerian, Zimbabwean and Kenyan legislatures while trying to articulate what it means to be "African", are faced with the contradiction of widely reported violence triggered by politicised ethnicities (what it means to be Luo, Kikuyu, Shona, Ndebele etc). We can look to Mahmood Mamdani's *When Victims Become Killers* (2001) and some of his previous work on the politicised ethnicities of the continent for further analysis. In other words these legislative events continue to expose the schizophrenic (im)balance between on the one hand individual, familial, ethnic, national, continental and racial identity and, human rights, freedom, choice and the increasing complexity of the human condition. In what ways therefore do these various stages of performance, of walking the tightrope and constantly confronting contradictions around sexual identities through sexual difference, come into even sharper focus in Neo's silent performance?

Pertinent and interesting questions arise from Neo's performance, especially in the context of the homophobic rhetoric that is presently sweeping its way through East and West Africa. These pertain to the ways in which the public reads the body; how the reading of the body is a process of "mapping"; the ways in which this "mapping" or "placing" determines power relations between the body being read and the people reading it; and ultimately, how this process of reading and mapping is upset or destabilised when the body that is subjected to this process is one that does not conform to assumed gender norms.

Neo's cross-dressing performance, if placed in context, accrues a particular symbolic value. The performance is in the middle of Tom Mboya Street in Nairobi, the capital city of Kenya. It is one of, if not the busiest, streets in Nairobi, peopled with hawkers, *Matatus* ("taxis" or passenger service mini-vans), and other mostly informal businesses. Tom Mboya was a trade unionist, government minister and rising political star who was assassinated in 1969. The symbolic resonance of this history of trade unionism, its ideas around freedom from "capital" is captured in a monument of Tom Mboya in the same street space of Neo's cross-dressing. Not lost to us is also the notion of the postcolonial city as a space historically designed with problematic gender divisions of labour – one that dates back to the inception of colonial modernity in Africa. The materiality of this history, its frozen presence within this monumental statue – itself a capsule of history – is clearly at odds with the informal market economy that is the mainstay of Tom Mboya Street. Moreover, in the background is the National Archives building, a visible yet symbolic colonial relic. It is within this context that Neo's performance is inserted into the uneven and uneasy entanglements between symbolic, cultural and economic capital.

The performance begins with Neo, whose hair is styled in a gender neutral and currently popular hairstyle, standing in front of the statue of Tom Mboya, with a heap of clothes at her feet. Neo's hairstyle consists of short dreadlocks on the top of her head, and a "fade" haircut (short back and sides/German cut). Neo is dressed in a white t-shirt and black pants, and rummages through the heap of clothes, with an expression of exasperation and annoyance, and selects a striped orange and white tight-fitting dress. Neo proceeds to change into the dress in a way that avoids showing more than arms and legs. Once the dress is on and the t-shirt and pants are off, Neo puts on a pair of black high heels. As a curious crowd gathers around, Neo proceeds to change clothes several times, alternating

between clothes that can be read as masculine and/or feminine respectively. In the end, Neo changes into black pants, a black and white striped shirt, a waistcoat, sneakers, a tie and a hat. Neo packs the rest of the clothes on the floor into a rucksack, puts on a pair of spectacles and walks out of the camera frame while in the process of switching on a transistor radio.

Neo's cross-dressing performance demonstrates the fluid boundaries of what the post-Freudian psychologist Stephen Frosh calls "sexual difference". For Frosh masculine and feminine categories whose social construction comes with regimes of power can be undermined by "simultaneously constructing and denying the fixed categories" (5). Neo's cross-dressing enables this crucial breaking down of distinctiveness, allowing us to ask, as Frosh does: "[H]ow can the material presence

of sexual difference be recognised without creating conditions under which that difference becomes an absolute state of affairs?" (10). In this performance a number of things related to the audience/public come into focus, as Neo's body transforms into a site of performed sexual difference.

Neo is silent during the whole performance, thus forcing the crowd to use the body as a map to figure out Neo's gender. This mapping process is difficult for the crowd though, as Neo keeps changing the traditional markers of gender: clothes. Neo's performance confounds while at the same time draws in the audience. While it comes across as a spectacle to some, to many, as we will see, this performance, in a Lacanian way, reflects its gaze back to a predominantly male audience, whose sense of what they distinctly identify as male or female is seriously brought into question. That an act as ordinary and as normal as dressing becomes the performance of the life of a body on stage is revealing.

The ease and fluidity with which Neo switches between male and female, by rapidly changing clothes, renders the process of mapping or reading gender on Neo's body quite difficult and thus makes it harder for the crowd to draw a conclusion about Neo's gender. The result is a variety of comments from the crowd about Neo's sexuality, and it is interesting to observe the ways in which the crowd's inability to assign Neo a gender role leads to questions about Neo's sexuality. Some members of the audience go on to draw from their repertoire of "knowledge" in a bid to read what comes out as particular, queer figures widely reported in the continent. Names such as "Semenya"[1] and "Audrey/Andrew"[2] can be heard. While the performance clearly challenges ways of reading dressed bodies and therefore assigning gender and sexual markers, it calls into question a particular imaginary about sexuality and gender. This imaginary, which assigns queerness particular distinctions of otherness, also elicits ways of disciplining the body that reflect problematic attitudes about medicalisation of queer persons: as the distinct voice of a woman in the audience says, "Huyu anafaa kuangaliwa" [this one needs to be checked]. This on-going commentary, initially unsolicited, comes across as unconscious but also continues to seek some kind of a consensus and opinion about exactly what distinct sexuality and hence gender is at stake: "Akivaa kama mwanaume, ni mwanaume, lakini matiti imetoka wapi?" ["If s/he dresses like a man s/he is a man, but where have the breasts come from?"]. While these statements are captured off camera, they are audible and the kind of affective responses to the performance – nervous giggling and laughter – clearly indicate not just the discomfort the performance is causing to the audience, but also how it continues to trouble what members of the audience consider "male" or "female".

Neo's cross-dressing performance therefore allows for a transgression of sexual difference.

> **The ease and fluidity with which Neo switches between male and female, by rapidly changing clothes, renders the process of mapping or reading gender on Neo's body quite difficult and thus makes it harder for the crowd to draw a conclusion about Neo's gender.**

To borrow the words of Frosh it undermines "the certainty of sexual difference… [in] this fixed form" which for Frosh is "a more promising avenue for progression to a less constricted set of gendered states" (123). As the performance reflects back in anxious and troubling ways to the audience, it opens up a range of questions. A male audience member asks: "What is your intention?" While recognizing the performative act of cross-dressing, questioning intentionality bespeaks the problematic connections between the apprehension of reality for the audience member and his subjective experience of masculinity. What the performance does is to trouble that connection and allow the audience to question their own assumptions about the material cultures of sexuality – those constructed through dressing, the performance that comes along with them and how the corresponding bodies are read. While the performance in fact underlines the notion of sexual difference, the fluid movement of the cross-dressing in fact allows us to reflect on what Frosh calls "the value of difference" (5). In this performance difference is acknowledged, while substantiated, with a value that should allow for a richer, more productive imaginary around sexuality. This imaginary is the bulwark against statements such as "people of your type", or questions from the audience such as "Are you active on

---

1 Caster Semenya is a South African Athlete and World Champion who was subjected to gender testing after winning Gold in the 2009 800 metres at the World Championships.

2 Audrey Mbugua, previously Andrew Mbugua is a Kenyan Transsexual whose battle to be legally recognised as a woman has been the subject of media frenzy in Kenya in the past two years.

male or active on female [sic]? You should be active on one side".

In conclusion, as we reflected on this performance the overarching idea of the "gaze" or "look" within and without the frame of Neo's performance was quite clear to us. Several levels of gazing or looking within the framework of performance make for interesting reflection. While Neo's performance mirrored back to the audience their own problematic assumptions around sexuality and gender (the masculine, feminine, the androgynous, and the queer) the camera, another audio-visual level of performance inflected its own deliberate framework of looking/gazing for us. The audience, the camera, the person behind it, Neo and we the contributors here provide varied "ways of seeing" this performance. It allowed us, within its own circumscribed yet strategic audio-visuality, a position both within and without the human actors on this stage. In which case we could peel off, as we do in this essay, the different levels of symbolic, political, historical and even economic capital accrued within Neo's cross-dressing performance.

Neo's cross-dressing performance, read as an event across a particular "time and space" invokes a critical debate on queer sexuality in Kenya, East Africa and around the African continent. Neo's performance continues to articulate what Binyavanga Wainaina, Kenyan writer and activist who recently came out in public calls "freeing our imagination"[3]. In a series of videos on YouTube, Wainaina makes this rallying call, seeking the kind of imaginary that Neo's performance articulates to its bewildered audience. In Neo's cross-dressing performance reading the body is rendered as an *imaginative* act that constructs particular subjectivities in the time and space in which it occurs. The performance not only "occupies" that particular space, it also elicits what Zethu Matebeni elsewhere calls "tensions between the space and what the work is saying"[4]. It is the kind of imagination which to borrow Frosh's words "is a potentially practical activity,

revolving alternative visions of experience, other ways of relating to the 'as if' reality of the world" (143).

REFERENCES

Eskine, Sokari & Abbas, Hakima. Eds. *Queer African Reader.* Oxford: Pamabazuka Press, 2013. Print.

Frosh, Stephen. *Sexual Difference: Masculinity and Psychoanalysis*. London: Routledge, 1994. Print.

Lundborg, Tom. Politics of the Event: *Time, movement, becoming*. London: Routledge, 2012. Print.

Mamdani, Mahmood. *When Victims Become Killers*. Princeton N J: Princeton University Press, 2001. Print.

Mutua, Makau "Sexual Orientation and Human Rights: Putting Homophobia on Trial." *African Sexualities: A reader*. Sylvia Tamale. Ed. Oxford: Pamabazuka Press, 2011. 452-462. Print.

Tamale, Sylvia. Ed. *African Sexualities: A reader*. Oxford: Pambazuka Press, 2011. Print.

3 See http://www.youtube.com/watch?v=kgJyDmQkIDQ
4 See http://www.academia.edu/5787060/Critically_Queer_Chromotherapy

THE TRANSGRESSIVE VISIONS OF JABULANI CHEN PEREIRA

by **Kylie Thomas**

Three young people stand entranced before a large, framed photographic print of a figure standing naked in the centre of a landscape.[5] The person in the photograph is in a mountainous place and stands not far from the edge of the rocky surface that occupies the foreground of the image.[6] On the left-hand side a road cuts through the earth and on the right a valley drops into the deep green undergrowth that forms the picture's darkest edge. The image is divided into light and dark with the person at the centre. Her hand covers her face but she does not appear ashamed. She stands on the edge of a precipice but does not appear at risk of falling. Her head is shaven and the skin of her upper arms tattooed so densely that parts of her skin merge with the green of the plants around her. The flat white walls of the gallery and the clothed bodies of those who are looking at the image are in marked contrast to the space and the figure portrayed in the photograph. At the same time the women who gaze at this image seem to be drinking it in, absorbing it, reflecting on it, recognising it.

The image is captioned *Indigenous*, a single word that carries a freight of centuries, a word that falls somewhere between descriptor and pejorative. Is it the landscape that is indigenous or the subject of the photograph? The framing offered by the critically queer exhibition makes possible one way for us to decipher the title.

◀ *Indigenous*, 2011

Jabu C. Pereira

Queer desire has been labelled as "un-African" and homosexuality has been castigated as western and "non-indigenous", as alien and deviant. Homosexuality, perceived as a threat to so-called "authentic" forms of masculinity and femininity and to heteronormative patriarchy must be uprooted and eliminated. Read in this way, the photograph asserts the indigeneity of queer subjects and the caption is both an act of claiming and a playfully transgressive joke.

At the same time, something in the construction of the image troubles this act of subversion. The woman's posture makes her appear at ease before the photographer's lens but the presence of her hand over her face complicates our reading. Her gesture is ambiguous and as we cannot see her face we cannot read her expression. Her body is presented to us but her face is hidden from view. The image seems to be asking us

> **She is not like anything we have seen before. And yet the women standing before her recognise her, she is like that woman who looks back out at us when we look into a mirror, she reminds us of ourselves.**

to consider what it would take for deeply entrenched ways of seeing the world to be overturned.

Is the photographer invoking the tropes of colonial ethnography (in which the bodies of Black woman and the landscape were conflated) in order to subvert them, or does the image present a decided break from these modes of representation? Are photographs, in spite of the relation between the photographer and the photographed always "taken"? Are photographic relations always asymmetrical?

Describing a portrait taken of her by photographer Robert Mapplethorpe, her friend and at one time her lover, Patti Smith writes, "When I look at it now, I never see me. I see us" (251). Smith articulates how photographs contain the time and space of the moment of their making and also how they can operate as a way to instantiate what is not there. The photographer is a ghostly presence in each image taken, absent from the frame, but present in the framing. More than this, in seeing both the photographer and the photographed in the image, Smith makes a case for understanding the photographic encounter as dialogic and as site of exchange through which both the photographer and photographed are constituted.

Theorist Ariella Azoulay affirms the idea that photographs bear witness to the shared event of their production and her work seeks to describe the ways in which photography can operate as a form of resistance to hegemonic forms of power. For her the photographic encounter takes place between the photographer, the photographed and those who, in the act of engaging with the image, animate its political potential (85). If we follow her line of reasoning, the three women photographed looking at Jabulani Chen Pereira's photograph also form part of the image and play a critical part in its production. The three watchers see the photograph in the context of an exhibition that overtly claims its queerness. The figure they engage with is not like the encounter they may have with the Venus de Milo or with a Henry Moore sculpture or a painting by Picasso of the naked form of a woman on the beach. She is not like Saartjie Baartman, nor is she like an ethnographic photograph depicting "indigenous" woman. She is not like anything we have seen before and in a certain sense she is someone we do not yet know how to see. And yet the women standing before her recognise her, she is like that woman who looks back out at us when we look into a mirror, she reminds us of ourselves. The question of how to read this image, I imagine, might form part of the conversation the three young woman share as they stand before the photograph, seeking to decipher its meaning and together making a space of queerness, a space of questions.

Attempts to unravel the meanings of this photograph are complicated further if the viewer sees the image with the knowledge that the person portrayed is transgendered queer activist Ignacio Rivera, also known as Papi Coxxx, queer porn-star and sex-

---

5 The photograph of the three people viewing Chen Pereira's photograph at the exhibition was taken by Collen Mfazwe and first appeared on the Inkanyiso website, 9 September 2013.

6 When I first saw this photograph I did not know the identity of the person in the photograph. I read the image as a photograph of a woman and have used the pronouns "she" and "her" to describe the person. I also read those facing the image at the exhibition as women. This exposes my own heteronormative gaze (even as I seek to undo it). The person in the photograph is transgendered and queer and prefers to be referred to as "they". I have maintained my use of the pronouns "her" and "she" to mark what I consider to be part of the power of the photograph – it makes visible the force of deep-rooted heteronormative and racist modes of seeing and at the same time challenges the viewer to radically rethink these.

In A Queer Time, 2013 ▲

Jabu C. Pereira

positive educator (Matebeni). Chen Pereira's photograph redoubles the queer effect of the figure of Papi Coxxx, amplifying the fluidity of a subject who refuses singular forms of naming and chooses to be referred to as "they". By casting Papi Coxxx in this way, as a naked brown-skinned woman standing in an African landscape, Chen Pereira surfaces the histories that haunt our radical refigurings of ourselves and draws connections between the lives of queer subjects across space and time. The photograph profoundly destabilises both how we might read the subjects of queer porn films made in the urban centres of the west and

how we see "native" subjects. In Chen Pereira's transgressive vision the multiple selves of Papi Coxxx are cast as indigenous and in this way the photograph unequivocally explodes the singular, hegemonic limits of this term.

Another portrait included in the exhibition works in a similarly quietly transgressive way. The portrait is an image of defiance, a photograph of a person with the body

▲ *Monumental*, 2013

Jabu C. Pereira

Loss I Series, 2012 ▲

Jabu C. Pereira

of a woman and the face of a man. As in *Indigenous*, the photograph subverts the conventions of ethnographic photography. Here the figure, seated on what appear to be bales of thatching straw intended for the roofs of homes in a rural place, wearing a brightly-coloured blanket traditionally worn by the Masai in Kenya and holding a beaded stick, adopts a decidedly modern pose and the expression on his/her face is unflinching. In looking at this image I have the sense that it is I who am seen by the subject of the photograph, that something has been turned around in the dynamics of power that ordinarily provide order to the experiences of seeing and being seen. The person sees me with eyes that judge, sizing me up, weighing up whether to accept me or refuse me, challenging me to be able to see beyond and outside of how I have been taught to see. "You who would condemn me for being who I am, I refuse your ways of seeing," he/she seems

to say without speaking. There is a terrible shadow of sorrow in his/her eyes, as though he/she anticipates those who will look with hatred, who will seek to kill him/her. It is a knowing look that does not underestimate the violence that waits in the future, a violence he/she seems to already know. In spite of this, the photographed subject lays themselves bare before us, offers themselves up to us as a gift that they know we are likely to misrecognise, to squander, to fail to protect. The photograph exposes the vulnerability of the human subject, how selfhood is embodied and as a result, always at risk.

The beaded necklace that encircles the neck of the person in the photograph draws attention to the part of the body that philosopher Emmanuel Levinas identified as the site of our

---

7 The person in the photograph is artist, writer and activist Neo Musangi.

most extreme vulnerability to the other and to the risk of violence (1996:167).[7]

The photograph on page 44 is captioned *Monumental* which could refer both to the scale of the print and to the struggle the subject of the portrait, Tiwonge Chimbalanga, has faced as a transgendered woman living in Malawi. Chimbalanga and her partner were jailed and sentenced to fourteen years hard labour for holding a marriage ceremony. Chimbalanga spent five months in jail where she was subjected to assault and psychological torture. The image of Tiwonge Chimbalanga is juxtaposed with three others by Chen Pereira that also form part of the *Critically Queer* exhibition. Each bears witness to the effects of loss on the families of women who have been raped and murdered as a result of their queer identities shapes my reading of this beautiful portrait.

By documenting families in mourning for their lovers, sisters, mothers and daughters who have been killed, Chen Pereira makes visible the shape of their grief. Many of the images portray the remaining family members who stand together in their family home. Such images powerfully convey the absence of the missing person simply by representing the family together and yet incomplete. One of the photographs in this series is a portrait of Roseline Morifi, mother of Andritha Thapelo Morifi, a lesbian woman who was stabbed in her neck with a braai fork and found dead in her home in Phola Park, Mokopane, on 29 June 2012. This portrait mirrors that of Tiwonge Chimbalanga discussed above. Roseline Morifi's face does not overtly express her sorrow, she is not weeping but instead appears frozen with grief. Her eyes convey the magnitude of what it is she knows, that which she cannot ever again not know, the horror of her daughter's death and the nature of the world in which such acts take place.

The way in which photographic practices can open spaces of and for solidarity takes on additional significance in relation to those realms of experience that are silenced and repressed. The desire to forge a bridge between private and public mourning, between the isolation of personal loss and the possibility of community, clearly forms part of the

photographer's intention in producing this series of works. And yet what is made evident as a result of the pain etched onto the face of the grandmother, a woman who seems to hold herself so tightly bound for fear of the enormity of the grief that would erupt if she were to let it go, is that the gulf between us is wide, there is no easy solidarity here, no simple way to recognise or appease her loss. "Try to look, just try to see," (82) Auschwitz survivor Charlotte Delbo wrote after her return from the death-camps, imploring us to bear witness and at the same time recognising the impossibility of the task of really knowing that which we have not endured ourselves. Chen Pereira's work travels into these spaces of fathomless grief. The photographs discussed here, like those by South African photographer Zanele Muholi, bring signs of mourning into shared spaces, such as that of the exhibition, leading us to reflect on both the isolation of grief and to think about how we might collectively mourn. We may wish to claim allegiance to those Chen Pereira represents, we may wish to claim we know them and that we feel with and for them. However, what these photographs seem to suggest is that there can be no facile form of solidarity, that looking is never enough and that there is work to be done. The task the photographs set for us is not just to think and to see differently but to make a world in which it is possible to live differently. Achieving this requires connecting what we see and what we do.

REFERENCES

Azoulay, Ariella. *The Civil Contract of Photography*. New York: Zone Books, 2008. Print.

Delbo, Charlotte. *Auschwitz and After*. Trans. Rosette Lamont. New Haven: Yale University Press, 1995. Print.

Levinas, Emmanuel. *Basic Philosophical Writings*. Eds. Adriaan T. Peperzak, Simon Critchley, and Robert Bernasconi. Bloomington: Indiana University Press, 1996. Print.

Matebeni, Zethu. "Queer(ing) porn - A conversation." *Agenda: Empowering women for gender equity*. 26 (2012): 61-69. Print.

Smith, Patti. *Just Kids*. New York: Harper Collins, 2010. Print.

Loss II Series, 2012 ▲

Jabu C. Pereira

IN TIME AND SPACE [8]

by **Neo S. Musang**

I.

To say that gender is performative is to say that it is a certain kind of enactment […]

(Butler i)

This thing that I am has no name. At least, not in the language of my people; the language of the people of my grandmother; those of my mother and those with whom I share similar identity documents. Pardon me if to claim a people is to implicate myself in an imaginary collective that can never be mine. Forgive what appears as a dis-connect from obvious modes of intelligibility. Pardon me if to use the pronoun "my" is to situate myself in a position of possession; a possession that appears as an exaggeration. But this is necessary.

What needs to be said is urgent.
One cannot be careless with form.

(Macharia 45)

I am an in-between and a beyond. I exist in-between normalised binaries and beyond those binaries. An in-between: something that does not quite sit in very well and when it does sit (if at all), it is somewhere between a pair of shorts and a pair of trousers. Too long to be shorts; not long enough to be trousers, like badly fitted harem pants. This is the in-between world of belonging and not quite belonging. But I belong to myself and to myself alone. Even if only sometimes.

I'm a lover without a lover /I'm lovely and

◀ *Criminalised-Desire*, 2012

Jabu C. Pereira

lonely/ I belong deeply to myself.
(Shire "34 Excuses for Why We Failed At Love")

I struggle to find a language and a form with/in which to speak of myself. A discourse has been availed to me over the years by others (see for example, Tamale 2011; Ekine and Abbas 2013; Murray & Roscoe 1998; Matebeni 2009; Halberstam 2005; Salo & Gqola 2006; among others). I could either choose to break my being down into palatable bits or speak in ways that are fragmented and incoherent. I falter and I, often, am startled by my own lack of ingenuity. My failed attempts at thinking outside the already-thought-through and my incredulity in theories even when I have, so often, found thinkers to think with. My lack of diligence in my people's language and the reluctance to dig through the archive to look for myself is not deliberate. It is an exhaustion of a particular kind.

Perhaps that language exists somewhere.
Perhaps there, too, is a form available for this kind of talk.
What could be truer, after all, than a subject's own account of what he or she has lived through?

(Scott 777)

The Akamba people of Eastern Kenya are my people. And sometimes are not. The thing that I am they call *tala*. They do not call me *tala*; it is the thing that I always was. A thing that I became; a thing that I am becoming. *Tala* is the thing that I am. But *tala* is not even a name; it is a description. To call myself "a thing" is to choose to exist outside myself. It is to look at myself with the eyes of another with an undeniable incongruity. To have to settle for "a thing" is to engage the limits of language; the desperate search for a naming word – a noun. To think of *tala* is to imagine a state of being and not being. Neither this nor that. This and that but not. I live as a description. Almost a question and often a condemnation: *"Sasa huyu naye ni mwanaume ama mwanamke?"*[9] I exist as a question mark: an inverted statement with a crooked mark at the end to signal incompleteness. A mark of waiting (for) − a dangerous waiting.

> This is not an assertion, nor an affirmation of truth. This is not an enumeration of something termed oppression or something experienced as such.
> **(Macharia 43)**

This is a story I crafted for myself. It was from the beginning a conversation with myself: the whole of me, all of me. I would imagine that it was always like this with me. Or maybe it was not. It became. I became what I chose, what was perhaps even chosen for me. I live here with myself and with bits of you, in-between. I have walked these streets before. It was not always like this. Or maybe it was; I just never noticed.

In these streets, men have touched me in ways I have not touched a man. In ways a man, too, has never touched them. But these same men have touched me −neither a man nor a woman. I have been told, on these streets, that I would be raped and possibilities of pregnancy thrown at me with overloaded hints at a forbidden termination. I, neither man nor woman, will carry the baby of a man whose name I do not know. A baby sired in the streets of Nairobi by a man whose face I choose to forget.

> They think rape as soon's they see you, and if they don't get the rape they looking for, they scream it anyway.
> **(Morrison 104)**

To be so often harassed in these streets is to signal the danger of your being: It is to take a risk with yourself. To continue walking these streets is to understand that your body presents itself as available for insults, advances, rape, for jokes. The body, presenting itself in privileging but vulnerable ways. It is to come to terms with what Keguro Macharia calls 'disposability' and the ever-increasing *killability* (Macharia, '*Gukira*'). More and more city streets are experienced personally and increasingly become individual zones of discard. One stages the uncertainty, precarity and (in)visibility of their queer body. Every day. But am I truly "queer" or was I queered? Life has to be lived or left.

> They have invented/ a new language/ It works a lot like/ the old language/ except the word/ fear/ has been replaced with/ life.
> **(Onsando "Teaching the Dead how to Live")**

II.

Performance art is internal and intrusive- it is like surgery without anaesthetic.
(Cohen "Thoughts on Performance")

In what language can one speak of an undefined pain? A pain so present yet not tangible: a pain that feels strange yet so familiar? Sometimes one has to find new ways of living with(in) fear. To find a new language: to experiment with words and thoughts when all has been said and nothing has been said (yet). There is a language to be found in a visible silence. To stand in the streets and draw attention to oneself is a possible − but not the only − language. It is one among many. It is to tell one's story without uttering a word. It is also to own one's pain and to immerse oneself into the matrix of danger. It is to put oneself "out there" as it were. It is to reclaim one's place in both time and space. To re-write their

---

8 This essay is largely experimental. It does not adopt any particular mode of writing: it is neither academic nor creative. The essay is based on a silent public performance by the same title done by the author in Nairobi, Kenya in June 2013. This essay seeks to find a language and a form for performativity; both of 'self' and space.

9 "Now is this one a man or a woman?"

own story and that of an imaginary "we". It is to mark space as defiled by the acts of one's existence in ways that are not allowed. *Please do not steal glances; look at me. All you want.*

> When you stand in front of me and look at me, what do you know of the griefs that are in me and what do I know of yours. And if I were to cast myself down before you and weep and tell you, what more would you know about me than you know about Hell when someone tells you it is hot and dreadful?
>
> **(Kafka cited in Brod 27)**

But what is it exactly that privileges acts of looking and how effective (if at all) is the grammar of looking itself? What does it mean to have city walkers stop to look at one whose "madness" is staged and for them to imagine it as such? The act of looking works both for the performer and the various publics and counterpublics[10] that quickly gather around them (Warner 2002). In this act one brings their everyday life into the spectacle of the city. This act is deliberate and requires deliberate considerations: calculated *tactics*. It is in itself an act of poaching

> **(de Certeau 98)[11]**

> Who has not [...] brought something performative into his everyday life?
>
> **(Cole 243)**

III.

Interview with Jabulani Pereira at the Market Theatre, Johannesburg, transcribed by Nala Xaba.

JABU: Okay Neo. Joburg to Kenya, Kenya to Joburg. Tell us a little about *In Time and Space* – the work that you did in Nairobi. Like the choice of location.

NEO: Um, so *In Time and Space* was a silent performance piece that I did in one of the busiest streets in the city, Nairobi, called Tom Mboya Street [...] this was part of my insertion into history. Tom Mboya was a liberation struggle fighter who was assassinated, allegedly by the Kenyatta government. So that space has always been – having a statue there and being so close to where he was assassinated – an important space of dissent and opposition to regimes of oppression.

JABU: So, within that space, can you explain the silent performance.

NEO: So, the silent performance was about… Well it was a dress-up-dress-down show. And part of the reason why it was silent was because silence, for me, was a metaphor for my own existence as a queer body within the space and also coming back into a space that I was before as a child and now coming back into that space as an adult and having to navigate those streets and constantly having to face verbal harassment – even when it wasn't thought of as harassment: kind of unsolicited commentary about my body and about my person.

So that silence was part of me not saying anything but also existing in that space in ways that I've existed over the last few months. Performing in that space where people have seen me before but also creating that space of performance that allows them to not make those same comments – to see me in a different kind of space, to see me in a different genre and see a performance for what it is, while

---

10 I use here Michael Warner's sense of a public as 1) "a concrete audience, a crowd witnessing itself in visible space, as with a theatrical public" and as such this public has "a sense of totality, bounded by the event or by the shared physical space." 2) the kind of public that comes into being only in relation to texts and their circulation. In this regard I refer to the circulation of the initial performance as a recording; as a text and the various audiences that it continues to create.

11 Michel De Certeau in *The Practice of Everyday Life* asserts that everyday life functions by means of "poaching" in the territories of others and recombining the existing cultural rules and products, which are influenced yet never fully determined by neither these rules nor products. 'Walking the city', de Certeau shows us, is not a way of appropriating the topography – the strategy – of predefined public space, but also a means by which the space unfolds and its relations are defined.

52

actually some of them know me outside that performance and they've seen the same person in that same space.

JABU: Some of the comments that people made were references to Semenya and people were very intrigued by whether you had two genital parts etc. Can you explain why the public responded more in relation to intersex issues?

NEO: I think one of the things about, not just Kenya, but one of the things about gender binaries is that if we cannot tell whether you are a man or a woman, then something must be *biological* about you, because there is no way that you could be neither of the two without really having a sort of biological anomaly. And so, intersex is an easier way to deal with gender ambiguity or gender queerness than to imagine that actually I could be trans, I could be gender nonconforming, I could choose to look a particular way.

And also, at the time, I mean the performance came at a time when there was a lot of talk about Audrey Mbugua [a transwoman who had come out in public to challenge the Kenyan government]. So that was an easier way of them seeing me through Audrey but also without understanding Audrey as a transgender person. So it was about genitals, it was about people wanting to know whether I had a penis or a vagina and which of the two was – which one I used more for sexual purposes.

Yeah, so that's an easier... But also it's a way that... It's kind of, intersex discourse creates a sort of safety because it's almost like saying there's nothing I can do about myself but at the same time it compromises who you actually [...] want to be and your freedom as a person to choose whatever gender identity you choose.

So it's a way of validating. Intersex allows people an entry – even when they don't

◀ *Somizi Ms Daveyton, 2012*

Jabu C. Pereira

> "
> **I'm doing that for the individual people who are struggling, for the intersex community, for the gender nonconforming, for the trans community in Kenya because I identify with those struggles as human beings, I get them.**

understand it. It's natural. It's more natural than choosing to not be either.

JABU: And lastly, in terms of this whole notion, in Africa in particular, about nationalism and where queer bodies fit into that. Do you have a particular view or perspective on this issue?

NEO: Yes. I mean, I think there was something about being in Joburg that allowed me a distance from state discourse. Even when I understood what having the current ANC government means for some South African queers; and having hate crimes; and having the government silent; and having people in government say very hateful things about queer people; I think still, I was a bit distant.

But being in Kenya and carrying this particular nationality has more informed my views on state violence. It has more informed my views on why I am not patriotic and why I choose to not be patriotic because I'm in this space where I was born into, I carry this passport that says Kenyan. And as nationalism requires us to be a particular imaginary collective that doesn't allow us to interrogate the many ways through which we are meant to be part of this collective, I cannot be part of it.

And one of the dangers for me is that, if there's an ideal of what Kenyan nationalism looks like then I don't fit into it and I'm destabilising that unity of the nation and relationship between the state and the national family. So I know, in myself, that I'm in this space but I know for sure I'm not part of the ideal nation that is religious nationalism, that is about morality that is because I'm deliberately immoral so I'm not part of that nation-state. So I'm not patriotic in that sense. I'm not going to die for my country or kill for my country. It's not mine. Because then in that way, by positioning myself as part of that nation, then it means I'm also ready to exclude a particular people who destabilise that notion.

JABU: And as a queer body what would you do for your country?
NEO: Um, I don't think there's anything I would do for my country, *per se*. There's something that I would do for queer solidarity across the universe. There's something I would do for an unpacking of oppression for everybody, which is not particularly located in my Kenyanness. It's much more located in individual freedom for queer people – whether I'm in South Africa, whether I'm in Kenya, whether I'm in Uganda – which is not nationally binding.

I mean there are queer people in Kenya who I know, of course they exist outside that idea of Kenyanness even when they are patriotic, even when they wear t-shirts [on which are] written 'Kenya' and when they claim to be "one" and defending their country against whatever else it is that is happening in the region.

But I don't think I particularly think of myself as – even when I get involved in queer work in Kenya – I'm not doing that for Kenya, I'm doing that for the individual people who are struggling, for the intersex community, for the gender nonconforming, for the trans community in Kenya because I identify with those struggles as human beings, I get them.

JABU: Thank you.

IV.

POSTSCRIPT

In this silent performance,[12] I employ Judith Butler's (2009) notion of "precarity" and Sontag's (2002) ideas on silence, through taking to a public space that which is deemed highly private: the act of dressing and undressing. While the performance situates the queer body as both an object of fascination as well as a threat, it destabilizes popular understandings of staged lives as distinct from lived experiences; the private as absent from the public; the personal as dismembered from the collective and; the physical as delinked from the sexual. This performance invites us to think of the many ways in which, in Butler's words, the "appearance" of gender is often mistaken as a sign of its internal or inherent truth and how the ways in which we perform gender becomes a negotiation with power at times taking the risk to undo or redo the norm in unexpected ways; a remaking of gendered reality along new lines (Butler 2009: ii).

REFERENCES

Butler, Judith. "Performativity, Precarity and Sexual Politics", *Lecture at Universidad Complutense de Madrid*. June 8 (2009). Web.

Butler, Judith. "Performative Acts and Gender Constitution: An Essay in Phenomenology and Feminist Theory." *Theatre Journal*, 40, 4 (1988): 519-531. Print.

Butler, Judith. *Gender Trouble: Feminism and the Subversion of Identity*. New York/London: Routledge. 1990. Print

Cohen, Steven "Thoughts on Performance". http://vweb.isisp.net/~elu@artslink.co.za/stevencohen/thoughts.htm. Accessed Feb, 09 Feb (2013). Web.

Cole, Teju. *Open City*. New York: Random House. 2012.

De Certeau, Michel (trans. Steven Rendall). *The Practice of Everyday Life*. Berkeley: University of California

---

12 "Silence is the artist's ultimate other-worldly gesture; by silence, he frees himself from servile bondage to the world, which appears as patron, client, audience, antagonist, arbiter, and distorter of his work" (Susan Sontag, "The Aesthetics of Silence" *Styles of Radical Will*, Picador 2002)

Press. 1994. Print.

Ekine, Sokari and Hakima Abbas, Eds. *Queer African Reader*. Nairobi/Oxford: Pambazuka. 2013. Print.

Halberstam, Jack [Judith]. *In a Queer Time and Place: Transgender Bodies, Subcultural Lives*. New York: New York University Press. 2005. Print.

Kafka, Franz *Letters to Oskar Pollak*. Liboch. New York: Schocken. (1903/1958). Print.

Macharia, Keguro "Miri ya Mikongoei". *Wasafiri* 22, 1(2007): 43-49. Print.

Macharia, Keguro *Gukira: With(out) Predicates*. http://gukira.wordpress.com/. Feb 05, 2014. Web.

Matebeni, Zethu. "Feminizing Lesbians, Degendering Transgender Men: A Model for Building Lesbian Feminist Thinkers and Leaders in Africa?" *Souls: A Critical Journal of Black Politics, Culture, and Society*. 11, 3 (2009): 347-354. Print.

Morrison, Toni. *Sula*. New York: Knopf. (1973). Print.

Onsando, Michael. "Teaching the Dead How to Live". Unpublished poetry anthology. (2014). Print.

Salo, Elaine and Pumla Gqola. "Editorial". *Feminist Africa*. Issue 6, Subaltern Sexualities. (2006): 1-6. Print.

Scott, Joan W. "Evidence of Experience", *Critical Inquiry*,   17, 4, (1991): 777-797. Print.

Shire, Warsan "Excuses for Why We Failed at Love" (Available: http://www.youtube.com/watch?v=f5CXxu7iZvk). Feb, 10 2013. Web.

Sontag, Susan. "The Aesthetics of Silence". *Styles of Radical Will*. New York: Picador. 2002. Print.

Tamale, Sylvia. *African Sexualities: A Reader*. Ed. Dakar/Cape Town/Nairobi/Oxford: Pambazuka. 2011. Print.

Warner, Michael. "Publics and Counterpublics". *Public Culture* 14, 1 (2002): 49-90. Print.

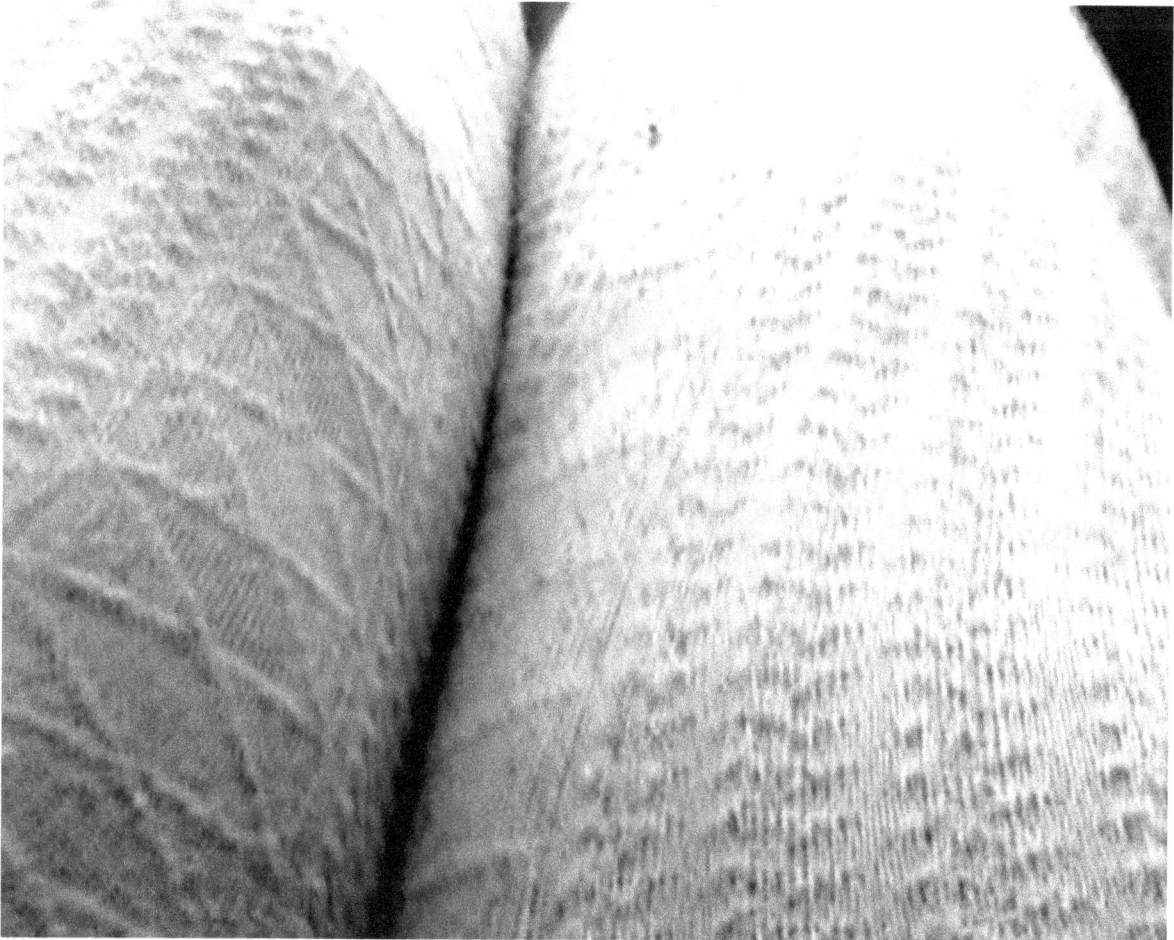

State of Emergency, 2005 Video 00:50" ▲

Dineo Seshee Bopape

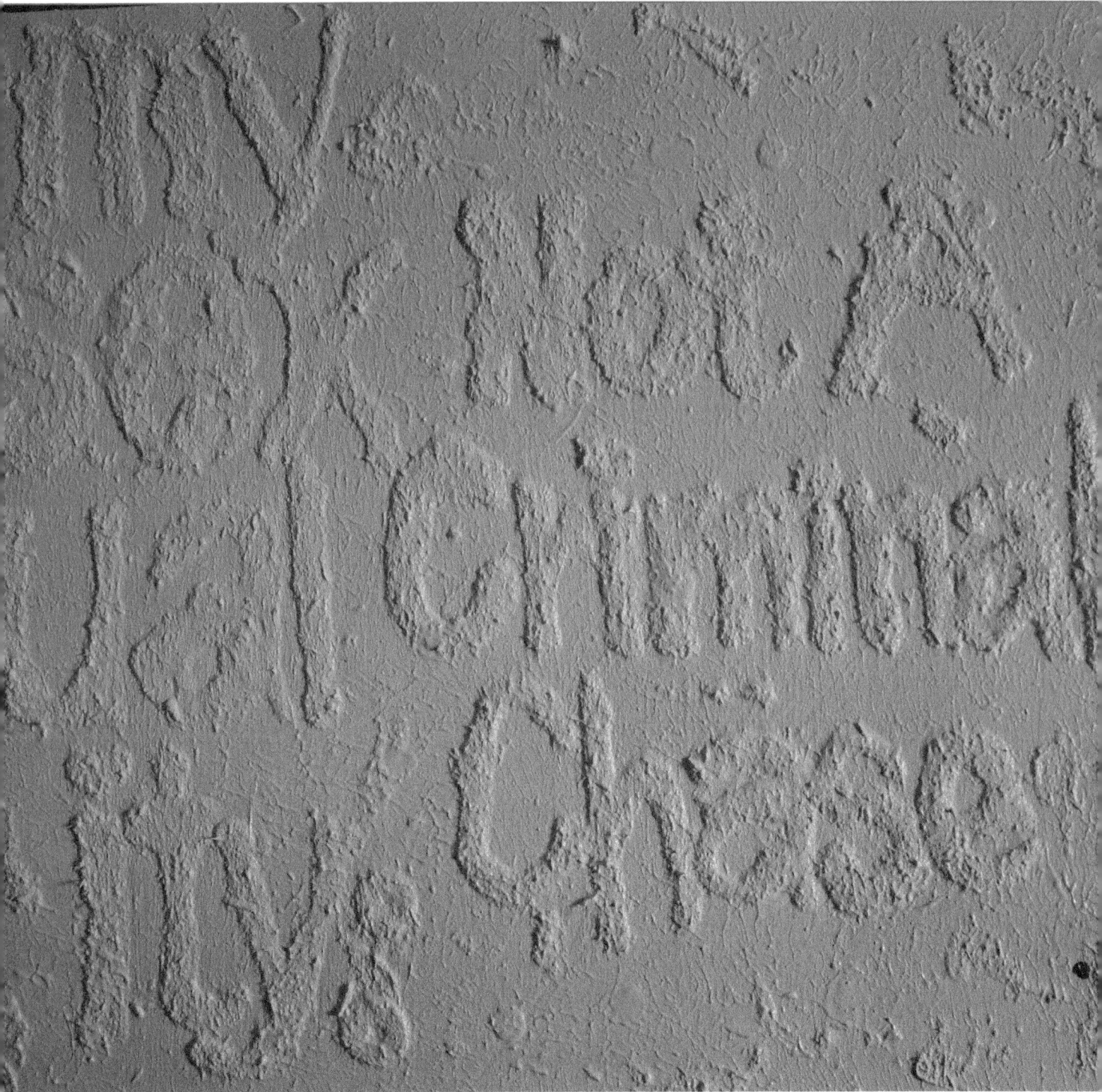

HOW ~~NOT~~ TO WRITE ABOUT QUEER SOUTH AFRICA [13]

by **Zethu Matebeni**

Always use the acronym LGBT in your writing. It sounds nice and it shows that you are inclusive. Do not spend much time explaining why you use LGBT. To help the reader, replace LGBT with gay. In later texts, put the word queer in the title. Like gay, queer does the same work, but sounds better. Don't worry that most South Africans do not use the word queer, they will all soon catch onto it. Your tone is very much about human rights and so it doesn't matter which word you use – all these are inclusive and they talk about one group of people.

Track the history of homosexuality or queerness in South Africa – start with prison writings – focus a lot on prisons. Prison was the space from where ideas came. It was also the space for homosexual passion. Some of your interlocutors will tell you "even after the achievement of the (South African) constitution, then, prison continued to be an imaginary space for the production of ideas about male homosexuality and its place in the history of the struggle".[14] Your main gay icon, Simon Nkoli,[15] was imprisoned and this is where his ideas of challenging racism and homophobia came, in the company of other men in prison. Mandela was also imprisoned. Even those in prison who were not homosexual, were homosexual because they were in homosocial spaces. This would apply to men in hostels too. They also had sex with other men. These were great spaces of community, creativity and passion.

Never write about a homosexual woman. Lesbians didn't really partake in the struggle for liberation. Gay men championed the struggle for gay human rights. Lesbians got off easy because apartheid laws, particularly the 1969 amendment to the Immorality Act did not really criminalise sex between women. Focusing on women wouldn't have made sense anyway because women can't have sex with each other. If a lesbian appears, make sure that she is just a criminal or a victim. She is after all, a crazy lesbian. There is only one kind of lesbian: the butch type. Someone like Getrude "Gertie" Williams is a good example. She was a lesbian gangster,[16] a real criminal. It's important that all lesbians are butch, and want to be like men or pass as men. And because of that, they are punished for their being – either imprisoned as Gertie was or raped or they are dead Black South African lesbians. Do not be bothered to write about lesbians who love each other, or the sex they have, no one is interested in that.

Always paint a picture that lesbians, particularly the Black ones, are from poor townships, are victims of rape and murder, and your writing and the money you will raise, will save them. Always mention "corrective" rape when you write about Black lesbians. Explain that because she is butch and looks like a man, she challenges masculinity. Therefore, Black men respond by using "corrective" rape to cure her of this.[17] The form of rape and sexual violation a Black lesbian experiences matters the most and warrants international attention

◀ *Not A Criminal Chäse*, 2014

Tyna Adebowale

> **Johannesburg or Cape Town are the major cities where the real gays and queers are. If you're not South African you keep coming back to Cape Town, around February and March. The weather is good and all the queers are out.**

because it is a "special rape" that is happening only in Black South African townships. You yourself have never been there because it is too dangerous. It is not necessary to write about white lesbians in South Africa. No one is interested in reading about them. Lesbians in other race groups also do not matter. South Africa is only known for its Black lesbians.

In your text, l,g,b,t people are all the same. They are all just gay. Writing about bisexuals does not make sense. They are after all, not really gay. They are sitting on the fence and wanting both worlds.[18] Rarely are they visible because in actual fact, they are heterosexual. In the acronym, they are just included because like gay people they are sometimes a sexual minority. If you want recognition from public health practitioners and policy makers, and to make a significant contribution, call them msm, men who have sex with men, or wsw, women who have sex with women (use capital letters). From these two groups, the world will learn a great deal about the transmission of HIV and AIDS.

Transgender people should never appear. Those are the confused lots. You should not be bothered to write about them because your feminist politics does not agree with the idea of transitioning. It's worse when a female wants to claim the privileged space

that men occupy. She or he, or whatever, has betrayed the fight against patriarchy because they have joined the enemy. In your writing always forget to use "he" for a transman because these pronouns are just too difficult or not appropriate. Anyway, she/he is not a real man.

The transwoman is not a real woman either. She was never born with breasts, even when she gets them. And she will never have a vagina. If she does, it is her privileged status of being a man that has given her economic access to surgery. She could never fully identify with your struggles. Anyway, it does not matter, she was not born a woman. Precisely because she became a woman, better to ignore her because she challenges your feminist stance. And such things as gender reassignment don't take place in South Africa anyway. Treat South African women and men as simple beings. They are either straight or gay. Don't get bogged down with precise descriptions of how complex they are.

Treat your readers to an experience in Johannesburg or Cape Town. These are the major cities where the real gays and queers are. You saw this when you attended the pride march. Readers would like to know that there are gays of all colours. If you're not South African you keep coming back to Cape Town, around February and March. The weather is good and all the queers are out. The village life in the mother city is the queerest place in the continent. When writing about this place, make sure to mention how safe it is for gay men to walk around at night topless. Be oblivious to the fact that you rarely see Black gays or Black people for that matter after hours in the city. Perhaps you can put a footnote that the city is safe precisely because there are no Black people.

---

13 This essay is inspired Binyavanga Wainaina's essay "How to write about Africa."

14 This argument is developed by Brenna Munro (2012).

15 See the collections of letters by Simon Nkoli edited by Shaun De Waal and Karen Martin.

16 See Chetty, Dhianaraj (1995).

17 This argument is presented and critiqued by many including Mary Hames, Mary (2011). Also see media reports by Kelly, Annie (2009).

18 Cheryl Stobie (2007) offers an extensive critique of the erasure (and yet presence) of bisexuality in South African literature.

Your other queer African characters must include refugees from the rest of the African continent. They come to South Africa to realise their queerness. Their plight in South Africa – unable to access asylum and papers – means they do not get jobs and are pushed to sex work; isolated from country folk and their homes, they do not get social support; violated by their own country folk and other South Africans because they look too queer – kwere kwere is only a minor detail. South Africa is their promised land.

End off your writing with a futuristic tone. Words such as dream, promise, freedom and queer should appear in your title, accompanied by the only highly celebrated black queer artist, Zanele Muholi's photography. South Africa has a wonderful constitution that has given access and rights to all lgbt people. It is the most progressive place in the continent and the world.

REFERENCES

Chetty, Dhianaraj. "Lesbian Gangster: Excerpted from Golden City Post and Drum Magazine." *Defiant Desire. Gay and Lesbian Lives in South Africa*. Eds. Gevisser, Mark and Cameron, Edwin. New York and London: Routledge, 1995. Print.

De Waal, Shaun and Martin, Karen, eds. *Till the Time of Trial: the prison letters of Simon Nkoli*. Johannesburg: Gay and Lesbian Memory in Action, 2007. Print.

Hames, Mary. "Violence against black lesbians: Minding our language." *Agenda: Empowering women for gender equity*. 25(4) (2011): 87-91. Print.

Kelly, Annie. "Raped and Killed for Being a Lesbian: South Africa Ignores 'Corrective' Attacks." *The Guardian*,12 (2009). Web.

Munro, Brenna M. *South Africa and the Dream of Love to Come: Queer Sexuality and the Struggle for Freedom*. Minneapolis: University of Minnesota Press, 2012. Print.

Stobie, Cheryl. *Somewhere in the Double Rainbow: Representation of Bisexuality in Post-Apartheid Novels*. Pietermaritzburg: University of KwaZulu-Natal Press, 2007. Print.

Wainaina, Binyavanga. "How to write about Africa." *Granta* 92 (2005). Web.

QUEERING QUEER AFRICA

by **Stella Nyanzi**

Queer Africa is much more than Michel Foucault and Judith Butler. It is lazy to always start our queer African narratives with either this French philosopher or his American compatriot. Departures to Jeffrey Weeks, Denis Altman, Gilbert Herdt and Peter Aggleton still fit into western hegemony over queer studies. Sprinkling the menu with Audre Lorde, Sonia Correa or Serena Nanda is a commendable effort but not nearly enough. Stretching this tapestry of authorities to include queer scholars with masculine names from the Global South outside Africa would be an exercise in missing the gist of my introduction. In fact queer Africa should transcend Marc Epprecht, Rudolf Pell Gaudio, Wieringa Saskia, Ruth Morgan and the bold Africanist non-Africans who generously contribute to the growth of knowledge about non-heteronormative sexual orientations and non-conforming gender identities.

The dominant role of predominantly white South African queers is as empowering as it is also colonising because queer Africa is much larger than this one nation. Miniscule articulations of alternative South African queers as only Black raped lesbians, or brown coloured effeminate men are important, but also gagging of varied ways of being queer and African. South African lenses cannot be the only frames through which queer Africans from the other fifty-five countries make meaning of our queer lives and realities. To queer "Queer Africa", one must simultaneously reclaim Africa in its bold diversities and reinsert queerness: two non-negotiable strategies that encapsulate the politics within this project. In this essay, I grapple with some complexities and possibilities within Queer Africa.

WHERE DO I FIT IN THIS QUEER WORLD?

With energetic passion and inquisitive curiosity, I insert myself into academic production of knowledge as a queer African scholar. Many citizens of the queer African communities that I engage with furiously kick against my claims to being a queer African scholar. "She cannot speak to us as one of us for she is not one of us," a butch lesbian once growled through a microphone, as her index finger pointed firmly at me, during an activist workshop in Kampala. "On whose authority do you speak for or about homosexual communities in Uganda?" a feminist academic asked after a presentation I gave in Cape Town. "Nothing for us without us!" a gay colleague passionlessly told me when I turned to him in frustration.

I needed to understand why queer Africans had problems accepting me as one of them; after all I was an active producer of queer African knowledge. If queer is indeed an open invitation to all of us opposed to essentialist patriarchal heterosexist heteronormative binary configurations of sexual orientations and gender identities, why did I repel queers? Whose right is it to determine who, what, where, when and how queer is? If queer is allowed to be queer, why are boundaries of inclusion and exclusion forcibly drawn – and usually based on essentialist readings by others of the perceived body under scrutiny?

◀ *Chromotherapy*, 2013

Stills from a performance by artist:
Selogadi Mampane
Photographed by Collen Mfazwe, inkanyiso.org

My body was variously scrutinised, read and found wanting as a queer African subject. But what is my body's first reading by others? What, in their reading, necessarily disqualifies me from being a legitimate queer African scholar? Is it my Africanness or my queerness that is lacking? Do others read me as well as I read myself?

I am a loud-mouthed full-bodied Black African woman with skin the colour of hot millet porridge. I wear brightly coloured three-piece dresses made of *kitengi* fabric with grotesque yet pretty African artistic patterns. My skirts are full and ankle-length. My blouses curve well across my big bosom. Headpieces sit as crowns atop my kinky dreadlocks that silently speak of resistance and defiance to strictures of feminine propriety. Uncritical readings of my body scream "African cisgender woman". My apparel is also stereotypically interpreted as signifying my heterosexuality and subservient monogamous marriage to a singular man.

Beyond race, skin colour, hip size and a simplistic interpretation of my physical presentation, I claim Africa as a geo-social political position. I am from the Buffalo clan of the Baganda ethnic group from Uganda in East Africa. My feminine clan-name is Nanyanzi. My bequeathed names from the ancestors are Basambye and Bategeeza. My Christian colonial name is Stella, although my mother also named me Diana after the first wife of Prince Charles. Our family name is Nyanzi. Stella Nyanzi, my public label, is both an affirmation and erasure of parts of who I am. While it affirms my colonised, Christianised, patrilineal and Africanised clan-leanings, it also invisibilises my feminised, ancestral and matrilineal heritage. While my African roots cannot be denied, my Africanness is variously questioned by my colonisation, Christianity and westernisation.

When I claim my space(s) as a Black African, woman, wife and mother, nobody contests this. However, the expectation is that as a Black African heterosexual cisgender woman and mother, I should stay in my place – on my side of the line. Because I am a Ugandan and a Christian, the first expectation is that I am heterosexist, homophobic, transphobic and bi-phobic. Queer Africans outside Uganda immediately associate me with the Anti-Homosexuality Act (2014). Thus I get quickly rejected from queer citizenship. And yet I persistently shatter these essentialist deductions and assert my claim as a queer African scholar. In doing so, I generate dis-ease, discomfort and antagonisms.

"Heterosexuals have no part in this queer world, for they are the oppressors," many LGBTI people object. Many others also insist that "queer" is a western paradigm through which neo-imperialism is sustained in Africa (Nyeck and Epprect 3-5).

WORKING WITHIN AND BEYOND THE FRAME OF THE LGBTI ACRONYM

Is there a place for heterosexual cisgenders in Africa's queer movement? Is there room for heterosexuals or cisgenders? When firm boundaries are drawn between homosexuals and heterosexuals, isn't this a simplistic re-styling of essentialist schisms? Isn't this another polarisation of binary oppositions – this time based on sexual orientation?

Where do bisexual people fit within the dual division between homosexuals and heterosexuals? Given the instrumentalisation of bisexuality as a protective decoy for some homosexual Africans living in highly homophobic national regimes, widespread neglect and denial of bisexuality erases a significant component of queer African subjectivities and experiences (Stobie). Furthermore, the neglect of those same-sex loving Africans who are bisexual by choice rather than circumstantially is a disservice to the growing queer movement in Africa. Bisexuality allows unpretentious recognition of polyamory; highlighting the problematic nature of simplistic readings of heterosexual presentations (Kajubi et al.). The shame and betrayal associated with bisexuality in the politics of queer identities can be tackled within a queer space that acknowledges the dynamic fluidity, movement and flux between and within sexualities, as well as the creative and enabling potential of individual African queers to mediate and move across sexual identities, partaking of diverse practices as they move along and between nodes on the continuum. One potential queer re-reading of all heterosexuals is their potential for bisexuality.

Many queer readings of sexual identities in Africa misread dynamic gender identities of bodies in flux (Jobson et al.). The limited fixing of transgender subjects into "only this" or "only that" definition is dangerous to the queer movement in Africa. Trans – whether transvestite, transgender or transsexual – experiences facilitate the destabilising of gender identities between the two polarised divisions of men and women, male and female, masculinity and femininity. The queer movement in Africa is much richer for having opened up spaces of freedom for trans men, trans women, drag kings, drag queens, mtf (male to female), ftm (female to male), as well as transsexual people. To this extent, we must celebrate specific local movements for freeing ourselves from the chains of heteropatriarchal gender binaries. However, where is the space for the trans person transitioning into queerness? Why must transitioning always and only be restricted to a change from one of the two gender categories into the other one? Why limit the transition only from male to female and from female to male? Where is the space for articulating gender neutral, gender fluid, gender dynamic and gender queer subjectivities and experiences? Why is the concentration around gender about being either male or female, but much less about being neither one of these, or indeed being both of them? Furthermore, why are trans experiences only validated when the gender non-conformance is bodily?

Intersexuality is a viable component of the queer African movement which easily mobilises empathies of heteronormative societal members (Swarr, Nyon'go, Munro). Because of anatomical disjuncture evident in some intersex individuals over the lifecourse, it is relatively easier for them to find the acceptance of heteronormative societal members. Unlike homosexuality, transsexuality and transgenderedness, blame for intersexuality is quickly shifted from the individual to nature, ancestors, divinities or God's creative abilities. Evidence of intersexuality – however complicated, be it hormonal, gonads, genetic, anatomic and physiological – is relatively more palatable to critics who contend against accepting the science of homosexuality,

> **Where is the space for the trans person transitioning into queerness? Why must transitioning always be restricted to a change from one of the two gender categories into the other one? Where is the space for articulating gender neutral, gender fluid, gender dynamic and gender queer subjectivities and experiences?**

transsexuality and transgenderedness.

Thinking beyond the loaded westernised frame of the LGBTI acronym, queer Africa must necessarily explore and articulate local nuances of being non-heteronormative and non-gender conforming. Language and language-ing beyond the English medium into diverse African languages and tongues is important towards queering queer Africa (see Leap and Boellstorff). Likewise fissures among Anglophones, Francophones, Lusophones and Arabophones must be sutured in and across the continent. Euphemisms, metaphors, similes, proverbs and riddles must be re-read queerly, alongside gestures, silences, erasures and invisibilisation.

Cultural and indigenous understandings of gendered spirits of ancestors who may possess individuals offer socially appropriate notions of handling fluid, transient gender identities. Queer Africa must reclaim such African modes of blending, bending and breaking gender boundaries. This necessarily calls for expanding the spaces for multi-spirited people, *sangoma*, traditional healers, spiritual guides and spirit mediums that facilitate local understandings of fluid genders (Nkabinde, Morgan and Reid). Likewise, cross-dressers, transvestites and other social groups that creatively transgress gendered boundaries of dress, clothing and fashion – whether across, within or beyond genders – offer poignant opportunities to study contemporary and/or historical modes of enacting alternative genders.

QUEERING SEX WITHIN AND BEYOND THE ANUS

While the study of anal sex is important to queer knowledge production, queer sexual practices extend much wider. The overt concentration on anal sex among same-sex loving men attests to the dominant androgynous positioning of men within the hierarchy of queer knowledge generation, advances of the anti-HIV/AIDS industry and the relatively more reticent roles of women, trans and intersex persons focusing on other aspects of queer life beyond disease and health. Vaginas, tongues, fingers, thighs, breasts, ears, feet, dildos, sex toys, whips, and ice-cream are but a small proportion of the myriad body parts and accessories that play vital roles in the queer African sexual scene. Queering sex beyond the anus is important specifically because many same-sex loving Africans never eroticise their anuses and rectums throughout their lives. Queer Africa must underscore the linkages between anal sex and heterosexuality (Lane et al., Kalichman et al.). This knowledge would complicate anti-sodomy laws that are narrowly translated as targeting homosexuality. Likewise, such queer knowledge would demand a nuanced approach to the efforts of the safe sex industry.

Queering queer Africa demands a widening of thematic focus for widening knowledge (Nyanzi). The canvas of possibilities demanding queer production of knowledge from Africa include relationships, pleasure, intimacy, parenthood, education, voice and expression, representation and visibility, housing and shelter, movement, migration, exile and asylum, employment, income generation, livelihoods, family, ritual, health, spirituality, religion, faith, ritual, violence, security and safety, nationalism, ethnicity, and globalisation. The methods of queering queer Africa necessarily demand innovation, creativity, multi-disciplinarity and a combination of academic scholarship, social activism and the diverse lived realities of local queer Africans.

REFERENCES

Jobson, Geoffrey A., Liesl B. Theron, Julius K. Kaggwa, He Jin Kim. "Transgender in Africa: Invisible, inaccessible or ignored?" *SAHARA-J Journal of Social Aspects of HIV/AIDS* 9.3 (2012): 160-163. Print.

Kajubi, Phoebe, Moses R. Kamya, H. Fisher Raymond, Sanny Chen, George W., Rutherford, Jeffrey S. Mandel, Willi McFarland. "Gay and bisexual men in Kampala, Uganda." *AIDS and Behavior* 12.3 (2008): 492-504. Print.

Kalichman, Seth C., L. C. Simbayi, Demetria Cain, Sean Jooste. "Heterosexual anal intercourse among community and clinical settings in Cape Town, South Africa." *Sexually Transmitted Infections* 85.6 (2009):411-415. Print.

Lane, Tim, Audrey Pettifor, Sophie Pascoe, Agnes Fiamma, Helen Rees. "Heterosexual anal intercourse increases risk of HIV infection among young South African men." *AIDS* 20.1 (2006):123-125. Print.

Leap, William, and Tom Boellstorff. (Eds.) *Speaking in Queer Tongues: Globalization and Gay Language*. Urbana and Chicago: University of Illinois Press, 2004. Print.

Morgan, Ruth, and Reid Graeme. "'I've got two men and one woman': Ancestors, sexuality and identity among same-sex identified women traditional healers in South Africa." *Culture, Health and Sexuality* 5.5 (2003): 375-391. Print.

Munro, Brenna. "Caster Semenya: Gods and monsters." *SAFUNDI* 11.4 (2010): 383-396. Print.

Nkabinde, Nkunzi Zandile. *Black Bull, Ancestors and Me: My Life as a Lesbian Sangoma*. Auckland Park: Fanele-Jacana Media, 2008. Print.

Nyanzi, Stella. "From miniscule biomedical models to sexuality's depths." Ed. Sylvia Tamale, *African Sexualities: A Reader*. Cape Town: Fahamu/Pambazuka Press, (2011):47-49. Print.

Nyeck S. N., and Epprecht Marc. "Introduction," Eds. Nyeck S. N. and Epprecht Marc, *Sexual Diversity in Africa: Politics, theory, citizenship*. Buffalo: McGill-Queen's University Press, (2013): 3-15. Print.

Nyong'o, Tavia. "The unforgiveable transgression of being Caster Semenya." *Women and Performance* 20.1 (2010): 95-100. Print.

Stobie, Cheryl. "Reading bisexualities from a South African perspective." *Journal of Bisexuality* 3.1 (2003): 492-504. Print.

Swarr, Amanda Locke. "'Stabane', intersexuality and same-sex relationships in South Africa." *Feminist Studies* 35.3 (2009): 525-548. Print.

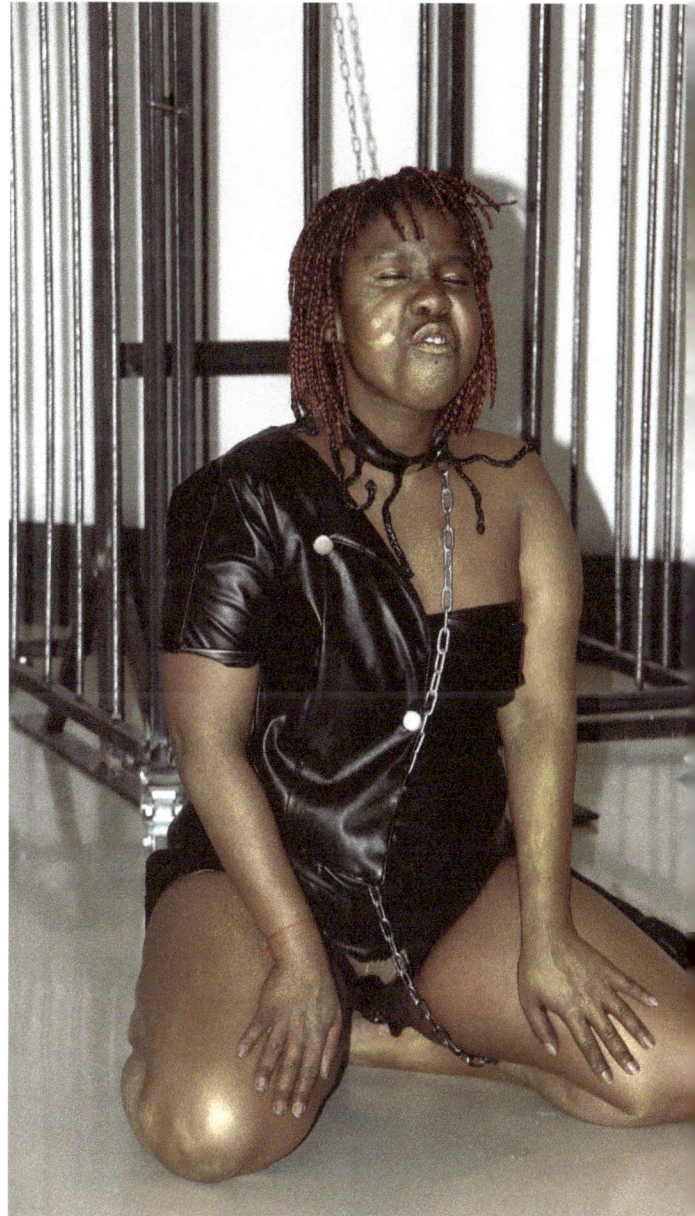

NEGOTIATING PERSONHOOD – WHAT IT'S LIKE BEING TRANSGENDER IN SOUTH AFRICA

by **Sibusiso Kheswa**

A choice to transition is extremely rewarding but one needs to be prepared to lose it all. One also needs a lot of support to be able to withstand challenges that come with transitioning. Even though my transition was relatively fast I was not exempt from the challenges that come with reassigning one's gender. Working in an office at an organisation advancing the rights of transgender people meant I had access to the internet and could easily do my research on gender transitioning. I guess being middle-class contributed a lot in fast tracking my transition; that is – I could get access to hormonal therapy, surgery, as well as follow-up on all legal documentation that identified me as who I am now. Instead of seeing a therapist once a month at a public hospital, I consulted a therapist privately on a weekly basis.

Hormonal therapy involves consulting with specialists; having blood tests done and buying hormones – all of which I could do because I had the resources. A significant number of transgender people go to the few state hospitals that offer these services. Groote Schuur Hospital in Cape Town, one of the few

◁ *Auntie TT*, 2012

Jabu C. Pereira

hospitals with a transgender clinic, says they currently have a waiting list of 20 years for gender reassignment surgeries. As waiting for twenty years was going to be impossible for me, I chose to take a bank loan, which I will have to repay over a long period of time. Having a job assisted in securing such a loan.

My experiences make me appreciate the struggles of those less privileged than me. One can only imagine the challenges faced by transgender and gender non-conforming people in African countries where homosexuality is criminalised. Of course, there still remains the conflation between homosexuality and transgender. The problem is that many people, including queers, policy makers, government officials and haters think gender identity and sexual orientation are one and the same thing. This was evident at the outbreak of the news of the "first gay marriage in Malawi". The media, particularly international media, created Tiwonge "the other gay man".

In its press release, Gender DynamiX, the organisation I worked with which housed Tiwonge when she was brought to South Africa for asylum, critiqued the view of Tiwonge as a gay man. The organisation was making a point that Tiwonge should be recognised as a transgender woman, given that she was already living and accepted in her community as a woman. In turn Gender DynamiX received a lot

> **Changing names on my bank account was a priority for me after transitioning. The more my face changed, the more I could not use my identity documents and bank cards at shops and the bank. Retailers would refuse to allow me to use that card, demanding that the female "owner" be present.**

of criticism as people could not think of gender as distinct from sexuality. There are links between transgenderism and homosexuality, but essentially the two are different. Being transgender is about a deep sense of a person's identity as a man or as a woman. It is about an individual's gender identity. Homosexuality is about attractions between people of the same sex, although these are often fluid. The links between the two exist in the fact that both fight against social and cultural norms and expectations.

South Africa's world-renowned Constitution promises rights and protection to all persons in the land, including gays and lesbians. It is from this premise that LGBTI activists litigated to change all discriminatory laws, including those directed at transgender and intersex people. The Alteration of Sex Description and Sex Status Act 49 of 2003 (Act 49) is the single most important law for transgender people in South African. It is a piece of legislation that recognises transgender people's reality. The law states that one is not required to have surgery to change one's gender markers legally. This means that medical treatment (hormonal therapy), as stated in the law, is sufficient to change gender markers on one's national identity documents. This is a significant step in realising the economic and social realities of many South Africans who cannot afford surgery.

Our enabling legal environment makes South Africa a place of choice for many persecuted transgender and gender non-conforming people who are seeking refuge from other African countries. Over the years, like other LGBTI organizations in South Africa,

Gender DynamiX has had to assist asylum seekers who flee their countries as they were targeted for violence or could be imprisoned because of their sexuality and gender identity. At Gender DynamiX we have internalised the Constitutional principles. We therefore have no choice but to extend a hand to anyone in need of our service regardless of their place of origin. In our experience, assisting one person has proven to be a project in itself as it requires a lot of resources. Our reality is that we have no capacity and there are no available resources to adequately assist. As a result, we ultimately have to refer to other social services and partner organisations that we work with.

Most of the time people's needs include seeking accommodation, food and jobs. All these are very difficult to secure as shelters are often segregated by gender. This makes it difficult for trans people to find a place to stay when they have found themselves homeless. The biggest need that most transgender people experience is having access to identity documents. Without an identity document, securing a job is almost impossible. Things are even harder for people who cannot speak any of the eleven South African languages. The implications for asylum seekers who were hoping for relief in South Africa are immense. Their imagination of a free and welcoming South Africa is tarnished as soon as they find themselves in our country.

For those foreign nationals who are able to go through the medical transition route, the challenge is that the Department of Home Affairs will not change their gender markers as Act 49 is only applicable to South Africans. The department's argument is that what can be changed is what is in the South African birth register only. So, if you arrive in South Africa and you are one person and transition here – your new gender identity will not be recognised because legally you are the original person you arrived as. This still needs to be resolved by our legal systems as this puts an

I am, 2014 ▶

Tyna Adebowale

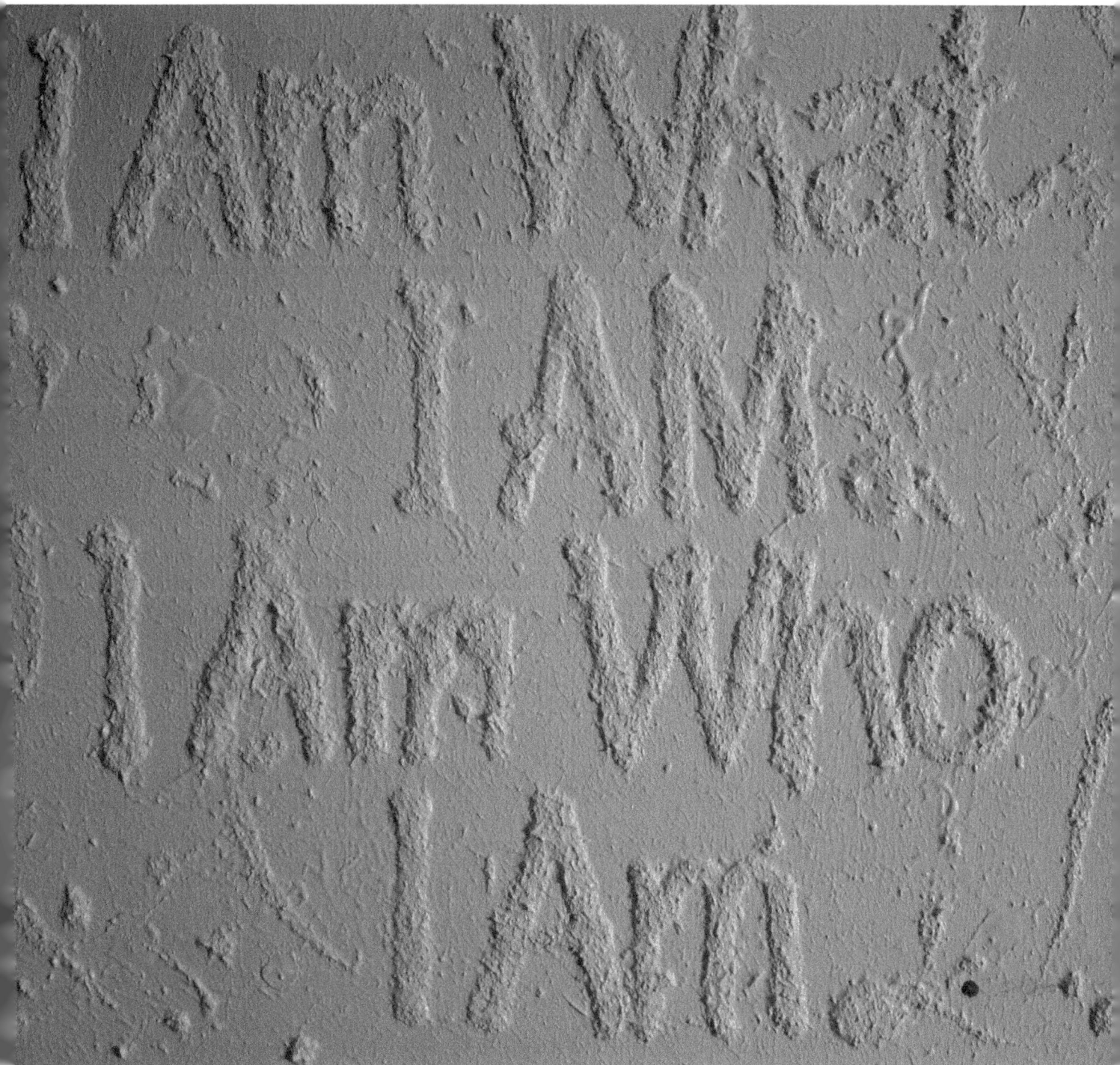

individual in a very difficult position seeing that changing gender markers at the person's country of origin will be impossible. The implication is simple and problematic: in many countries in Africa transgenderism is confused with homosexuality and homosexuality is criminalised. This means that there is no possibility of making changes to legal documents in the person's country of origin.

At Gender DynamiX we have found that the most difficult place for transgender and gender non-conforming people to access in this country is the Department of Home Affairs. Many times we have had to hold our members' hands as we walked them to the long queues at Home Affairs to apply for documents. In many cases this support is necessary as members have been pushed to the back of the queue because of their ambiguous gender presentation. It has to be noted that something as simple as queuing is still quite gendered. It appears that within the confines of the Home Affairs queue that homophobia and transphobia continues to prevail.

Many LGBTI asylum seekers who have come to South Africa seeking acceptance and safety, still have to face the attitudes that they thought to leave behind. Since her arrival in Cape Town, Tiwonge has already been attacked twice by other Malawians who accuse her of disgracing their country. Tiwonge has been living as a woman all her life and has been in South Africa for more than a year, but she has not started with her medical transition because she does not yet have the adequate papers. As in many countries, one needs to produce an identity document to access most things, including going to the hospital and opening a bank account.

Changing names on my bank account was a priority for me after transitioning. The more my face changed, the more I could not use my identity documents and bank cards at shops and the bank. Retailers would refuse to allow me to use that card, demanding that the female "owner" be present. To make any changes on your bank account you need an identity document. Even though Act 49 allows for the application of changing gender markers after medical OR surgical transition, its implementation is still very inefficient and inadequate. While waiting a minimum of nine months for the updated identity document, one's life freezes. Practically it means one cannot travel; go to the hospital; drive a vehicle; vote; enter any contract including employment applications; and get credit or use any service that requires one to produce an identity document. These may seem to be simple things, but they matter significantly in recognising the value of personhood and ensuring that all people have dignified lives.

Self Portraits: *Crucible* ▶
Acrylic on Canvas, (150 x 100 cm) 2010
A vessel for melting and calcining
a substance at a very high temperature;
a severe test of faces.

Milumbe Haimbe

CONTRIBUTING AUTHORS AND ARTISTS

TYNA ADEBOWALE grew up in Edo state in Nigeria, where she got most of her basic education. Lagos was where she found deeper context and art spaces like the Centre for Contemporary Arts Lagos (CCA) that expands critical representations in the arts. She now lives in Lagos and has started on a creative process to redefine her art practice(s).

UNOMA AZUAH teaches writing and literature at Lane College in Jackson, TN. USA. Her novels, *Sky-high Flames* and *Edible Bones* have won multiple awards including the Urban Spectrum award and the Aidoo-Snyder book award. Additionally, Unoma has been recognized by *The Journal of Blacks in Higher Education* as well as listed as one of the Top Professors at affordable private small colleges and universities in the US. *On Broken Wings: an anthology of best contemporary Nigerian poetry*, her latest edited work has just been released.

DINEO SESHEE BOPAPE was born in 1981, on a Sunday. If she were Ghanain, her name would be Akosua/Akos for short. During the same year of her birth, the Brixton riots took place; two people were injured when a bomb exploded in a Durban shopping centre; Bobby Sands dies; MTV is launched; the Boeing 767 makes its first airflight; Umkonto we Sizwe performs numerous underground assaults against the apartheid state. Winnie Mandela's banishment orders are renewed for another 5 years; in the region of her birth, her paternal grandmother dies affected by dementia; that year millions of people cried and billions of people laughed... The world's population was then apparently at around 4.529 billion... Today Bopape is one amongst 7 billion - occupying multiple adjectives.

MILUMBE HAIMBE was born in Lusaka, Zambia. She has a Bachelor's Degree in Architecture attained from the Copperbelt University, and also holds a Master's Degree in Fine Arts obtained from the Oslo National Academy of the Arts in Norway. Drawing on a background of painting, Milumbe's current art practices are based in digital illustration, including sequential art as an intermedial process that combines and integrates illustrations and written texts into narratives. Milumbe asserts that these intermedial concerns are related to intercultural issues, with a focus on the forms of representation of cultural minorities within the context of popular media. She has exhibited her work in numerous shows both locally and internationally, including FOCUS 10 – Art Basal in Switzerland, and is an alumnus of the Art Omi International Artist's Residency in New York. She has recently been selected to participate in the Biennale for Contemporary African Art in Dakar for 2014.

JACK HALBERSTAM is Professor of American Studies and Ethnicity, Gender Studies and Comparative Literature at the University of Southern California. Halberstam is the author of five books including: *Skin Shows: Gothic Horror and the Technology of Monsters* (Duke UP, 1995), *Female Masculinity* (Duke UP, 1998), *In A Queer Time and Place* (NYU Press, 2005), *The Queer Art of Failure* (Duke UP, 2011) and *Gaga Feminism: Sex, Gender, and the End of Normal* (Beacon Press, 2012) and has written articles that have appeared in numerous journals, magazines and collections.

SIBUSISO KHESWA is the advocacy coordinator at Gender DynmaiX in Cape Town. S'bu has been working in the South African LGBTI sector since 2002, where he has held positions at Gay and Lesbian Memory in Action (GALA), Forum for the Empowerment of Women (FEW), and the Lesbian and Gay Equality Project. He has worked on various research projects, public education and oral history projects. His works includes co-writing a chapter in a book: *Tommy Boys Lesbian Men and Ancestral Wives: Female Same-Sex Practices in Africa*. He also co-directed *Breaking out of the box*, a documentary film on black lesbian lives.

JACQUELINE MARX is a research psychologist and senior lecturer at Rhodes University and a collaborator in the SARChi Critical Studies in Sexualities and Reproduction research programme. Her recent research deals with the politics of homosexual visibility. It examines the role of race and gender in exacerbating and diminishing homosexual visibility, and considers the circumstances in which invisibility is desirable.

ZETHU MATEBENI is a Researcher at the Institute for Humanities in Africa (HUMA) at the University of Cape Town. She has worked for many years on issues of sexuality and gender, in particular within the lesbian, gay, bisexual and transgender movement in South Africa and currently Swaziland. Zethu is an activist, academic and documentary filmmaker who has published on queer issues, gender non-conformity, lesbian issues, popular culture, HIV/AIDS and sexual identities.

NEO MUSANGI is a gender non-conforming feminist researcher and performer based at the British Institute in Eastern Africa, Nairobi-Kenya. Their research interests include: War, militarism/militarization and nationalism, toilet politics and urbanity, gender and body materiality, sexuality and citizenship.

MPHATI MUTLOANE is currently registered as an LLM student at UCT. She holds BA Law and LLB degrees from the University of the Witwatersrand. She specialises in Public law specifically constitutional law and human rights, and the intersection between law and society.

KELEBOGILE NTLADI was born in Soweto and raised on the East of Johannesburg. Lebo schooled at The College of Cape Town and studied Fine Arts. In 2010 she was involved with Keleketla library, an inter-disciplinary, independent library and media arts organization based in the heart of Johannesburg as a volunteer photographer, which inspired studies in Photography at the Market Photo Work Shop.

STELLA NYANZI is a medical anthropologist based at the Makerere Institute of Social Research (MISR) in Uganda. Her research interests are sexualities, reproductive health, health policy, youths and children, alternative healing therapies, and culture. Stella has research experience in conducting ethnographic fieldwork and qualitative research in Uganda, The Gambia and more recently Tanzania.

CHRISTOPHER OUMA is a Lecturer at the Department of English at the University of Cape Town. Chris received his doctorate from Wits University where he worked as an Andrew W Mellon mentee at the department of African literature. His research interests and publications revolve around popular culture, the representation of Childhood and its connections to Postcolonial studies and Contemporary or new Diasporic African identities. He lectures and gives seminars on East, West and South African literatures and literatures of African Diaspora.

JABU PEREIRA is the Executive Director and founder of Iranti-Org since June 2012. Before founding Iranti-org, Jabu worked at Soul City and the Foundation for Human Rights advocating for the rights of marginalised groups. Jabu has a Masters degree in Museum Studies from New York University and largely uses curatorial space as a form of direct action in using visual art to express social change.

KYLIE THOMAS teaches and writes about the history and theory of photography; contemporary South African art and visual culture; the history and representation of the HIV/AIDS epidemic; violence during and after apartheid; and about visual activism. Her book, *Impossible Mourning: Visuality and HIV/AIDS after apartheid* has been published by Bucknell University Press in the United States and is forthcoming with Wits University Press in South Africa in 2014. She edits an interdisciplinary journal of African Studies, *Social Dynamics* and is part of the editorial collective of the journal *Feminist Africa*. She has taught in the Fine Art Department at Rhodes University and is now working in the Department of English at the University of Stellenbosch.

SELOGADI NGWANANGWATO MAMPANE describes them-self as a Queer, radical, Africanist, feminist, a human rights activist, academic and artist working towards being a peacebuilder, specifically around issues of sex, gender and race. Selogadi has obtained a BA (Drama) and a BA (Drama and Film) Honours from the University of Pretoria in which their research focused on the representation of 'Black, female-bodied people' as a victims of sexual violence, in contemporary South African theatre. Selogadi is currently completing their Masters in Drama at the University of Pretoria, focusing on 'female-bodied masculinity'.

IRANTI-ORG
Aunti TT, 2012
Materials: Tecco matt with archival ink.

DINEO SESHEE BOPAPE
Light Switch, 2013
Video 1:45"

DINEO SESHEE BOPAPE
State of Emergency, 2005
Video 00:50"

TYNA ADEBOWALE
In The Closet Series, 2012
Copies of Paintings from Lagos.
This series brings to the fore, the oppression of desire, the limitations of freedoms in Nigeria.

JABU C. PEREIRA
Criminalized-Desire, 2012
Tecco matt with archival ink.
Using expired roles of film, brings the "noise" of the image and the composition into dialogue.

SELOGADI MAMPANE
Chromatherapy, 2013
Performance and Residue.
Within the culture of violence that plagues LGBTI people in South Africa. Chromotherapy explores how the black body is policed, violated and objectified.

Self Portraits: *Wallpaper* ▶
Acrylic on Canvas, (150 x 100 cm) 2010
I see so many shapes in the patterns of the wallpaper. How about those childhood musings don't come back to haunt me?

Milumbe Haimbe

www.ingramcontent.com/pod-product-compliance
Lightning Source LLC
Chambersburg PA
CBHW041428270326
41932CB00031B/3500